IFISM
The Complete Works of Òrúnmìlà
Volumes Eight and Nine

The Odus of Irosun
And
The Odus of Owanrin

C. Osamaro Ibie

ATHELIA HENRIETTA PRESS, INC.
Publishing In The Name Of Òrúnmìlà
1194 Nostrand Avenue, Brooklyn, N.Y. 11225 U.S.A.
Tel: (718) 493-4500 - Fax (718) 467-0099
Tel: (718) 774-5800 - Fax (718) 774-5800

Interior design: Roland Francis
Cover design: David O'Donnell

Printed in the United States of America.

ISBN 1- 890157- 09 - 0

ATHELIA HENRIETTA PRESS, INC.
Publishing In The Name Of Òrúnmìlà
1194 Nostrand Avenue, Brooklyn, N.Y. 11225 U.S.A.
Tel: (718) 493-4500 - Fax (718) 467-0099
Tel: (718) 774-5800 - Fax (718) 774-5800

Other titles by C. Osamaro Ibie

Ibie, C. Osamaro
IFISM: THE COMPLETE WORKS OF ÒRÚNMÌLÀ
251PP. 2 b/w, 11line, Illust. Cloth

Ibie, C. Osamaro
IFISM: THE COMPLETE WORKS OF ÒRÚNMÌLÀ
VOL. 2-THE ODUS OF EJI-OGBE
HOW MAN CREATED HIS OWN GOD
242pp. 5 b/w, 41line, Illust.

Ibie, C. Osamaro
IFISM: THE COMPLETE WORKS OF ÒRÚNMÌLÀ
VOL. 3-THE ODUS OF OYEKU-MEJI
101pp. 1 b/w

Ibie, C. Osamaro
IFISM: THE COMPLETE WORKS OF ÒRÚNMÌLÀ
VOL. 4-THE ODUS OF IWORI
172pp. 1 b/w

Ibie, C. Osamaro
IFISM: THE COMPLETE WORKS OF ÒRÚNMÌLÀ
VOL. 5-THE ODUS OF IDI
144pp. 1 b/w

Ibie, C. Osamaro
IFISM: THE COMPLETE WORKS OF ÒRÚNMÌLÀ
VOL. 6 & 7-THE ODUS OF OBARA AND OKONRON
153pp.

IFISM
The Complete Works of Òrúnmìlà
Volume Eight
The Odus of Irosun

Volume Nine
The Odus of Owanrin

Table of Contents

IFISM
The Complete Works of Òrúnmìlà
Volume Eight
The Odus of Irosun

IFISM
The Complete Works of Òrúnmìlà
Volume Nine
The Odus of Owanrin

Chapter 3
Owanrin-Iwori

Chapter 4
Owanrin-Si-Idi
Owanrin-Sidin

Chapter 5
Owanrin-Obara
Owanrin-Kpalaba
Owanrin-Kpajibasude
Owanrin-Oloba

Chapter 6
Owanrin-Okonron

Chapter 7

Owanrin-Irosun
Owanrin-Logbon
Owanrin-Ewi

Chapter 8

Owanrin-Ogunda
Owanrin-Ogunrere
Owanrin-Ologbon

Chapter 9

Owanrin-Osa
Owanrin-Pisin
Owanrin-Ga-Asa

Chapter 10

Owanrin-Etura
Owanrin-Elejigbo

Chapter 15
Owanrin-Ofun

Index

About the Author

Mr. C. Osamaro Ibie was born in the defunct Benin Empire's capital City of Benin in Mid- Western Nigeria on the 29th of September, 1934 to Chief and Mrs. Th ompson Ibie Odin.He hailed from a Christian family.When his naming ceremony was, however being performed eight days after his birth, experts in the esoteric analysis of newly born infants, with special reference to the late Chief Obalola Adedayo, who confirmed to journalists when Ifism: *The Complete Works of Òrúnmìlà Vol. One* was being launched in 1987, predicted that God created the infant as a servant to Òrúnmìlà, God's own servant and divinity of wisdom, and that the world was going to know about Òrúnmìlà and the distorted, falsified and fabricated truth about the true nature of the one and only good God through the infant whose future problems and prospects were being analyzed. In fact, Chief Obalola confessed that he himself wondered why Òrúnmìlà left the whole of Yorubaland, which was his base, to come to Benin, which he first visited but could not reside in, to pick his *viva voce*.

According to the author's father the augury was totally ignored as farfetched because the man was talking to a Christian family who could not imagine any connection with Òrúnmìlà.

The author went through his primary and secondary education in Benin City, during which he generally operated as a man-server in the Catholic Church. In 1947, he joined some of his friends to enlist in the priesthood of the Catholic Church, but his father intervened with the Bishop to insist that his son was not cut out for the Christian priesthood, and the Bishop deferred to the wish of his father by releasing him.

Upon the completion of his primary and secondary education, the author was employed in the Nigerian Federal Public Service where he rose from the post of a Clerical Officer to the lofty position of an Executive Officer in 1959. At the same time, he won a Federal Government Scholarship to read Economics in London. He went to London in 1960 and obtained a Second Class Honor Degree in both Strathclyde, Glasgow and the University of London.

He returned to the Nigerian Federal Public Service where he was appointed as an Assistant Secretary, becoming Deputy Permanent Secretary in 1973 and Permanent Secretary in 1975.

He was appointed as a member of the Nigerian Economic and Finance Committee on the same year, which was charged with the management of the Nigerian economy. At the same time, he was appointed as a member of the Nigerian Government delegation to the intergovernmental consultative conference between the American and Nigerian governments, on which he served between 1976 and 1980.

Between 1980 when he retired voluntarily from the Nigerian Federal Public Service, and 1989, he operated exgratiation as an economic analyst; writing many newspaper articles on the categorical and hypothetical imperatives of economic policy and management. He also addressed several public and private sector institutions on the directions of economic policy, including the Nigerian Institute of Bankers, the Manufacturers Association of Nigeria, Nigerian Institute of Strategic Studies, several tertiary educational institutions, etc.

From 1985 and to the present, he has been serving as a member of the governing Council of the Federal Government owned University of Benin, in Edo State. Since his retirement from the Civil Service in 1980, he has actively engaged in business in the private sector. He was in 1992 awarded an Honorary Fellowship of the Institute of Administrative Management of Nigeria (FIAMN - Hon.) and recognized as a Certified and Distinguished Administrator (CDA).

Dedicated to
Roland Francis

The Late Babalawo Roland Francis
Orunmila's Ambassador and Plenipotentiary Extraordinaire
in the Western Hemisphere

A Father With A Difference

Chief Thompson Ibie Odin, the late Osague of Benin was born on the 3rd of October 1903 in Usen, a town seventy-two kilometers from Benin. He was the great grand son of Ezomo Henua, the great military commander-in chief of king Ozolua's armed forces of the Benin from 1914 to 1922. Thereafter, he learned many trades until Chief Agbeleri's son-in-law, Mr. Josiah Amadasun (who died in August 1995 in his early nineties) who was married to Ifamuseye, got him employed at the Resident's Office in Benin in 1928.

He worked in both the District and Resident Offices until 1951 when he voluntarily retired from the public service. In spite of the fact that he was brought up in a pagan home, he was however, ensnared by the appeal of the Anglican religion to become a Christian by stealth, because he dared not allow Chief Agbeleri, his master, to know about his allurement to the White man's religion.

He befriended a woman called Imaruagheru in 1929, who became pregnant and as a result of which he married her. She gave birth to my eldest brother on the 21st of May, 1930. He subsequently parted ways with his wife when my brother was nine months old, to be raised by my father's mother, who was from the royal family, until he married my mother, who continued to bring up my brother after the death in 1935 of my paternal grandmother, soon afterwards I was born.

My father continued with his Christian faith until circumstances compelled him to meet Chief Obalola, first in the home of Agbeleri, but later on in the mid-twenties, when the man prepared the way for him to be able to secure a civil service job in 1928, the year he got his own Ifá. The impact that Ifa made on his life made him gradually disengage from Christianity during the Second World War. Were it not for that conversation to Ifism, I am sure that I would not have been brought within hailing distance of Ifism, and the corpus of knowledge which have thus far been imparted through me to the world might have been a nonevent. My father's Ifá was Eji-Ogbe, the king of the sixteen Olodus of Òrúnmìlà. Following his retirement from public service in 1951, he spent the remaining forty years of his life as a practicing Ifá priest on a part-time basis. After my mother, he subsequently married five other women between 1939 and 1976, which gave him a total of thirty-one children, ninety grandchildren and four great grand children by the time he died in February 1990.

Unfortunately, proficient as my father was as an Ifá priest, I did not give myself the opportunity of learning from him, because I was during his active years, still enchanted by the synthetic and exotic appeal of Christianity, until experience taught me the lesson in 1969. My father acquired his knowledge by establishing an Ifá club which included among others; Chief Obalola, Pa Olodipe, Chief Aigbedion and Pa Iyamu Eruogun, with himself as Secretary. I have always recalled Òrúnmìlà's dictum that the worst thing that can happen to anyone is to be brought to the world by the wrong parents and in the wrong environment. Perhaps the most rewarding privilege endowed on me by God, was to give me the benefit of my parentage and their milieu. I sometimes wonder whether I deserve them. I have a consolation though. I was able to requite their investment in me in terms of the satisfaction I eventually gave them in kind. One major source of pride to my father - not my mother who strove through thick and thin to keep me alive, to outlive her which was her greatest pleasure - was that he was the father to the third Benin son to rise to the position of Permanent Secretary, after Mr. Matthew Asemota Tokunboh (my mother's first cousin) and Oba Erediauwa, in the Nigerian Federal Public Service. Before then, he had derived inestimable satisfaction from the fact that he prepared his son to win a Federal government scholarship for his tertiary education in the United Kingdom, during the sunset of colonial administration in Nigeria. He was the very quintessence of humanitarianism because he was always prepared to use whatever he had and knew to assist his fellowmen. He was a man of modest means, but during my upbringing between 1940 and 1953, I never knew him to refuse to oblige when anyone sought his assistance. I have only striven over the years to follow his examples in my attempt to be benevolent and benign in my interactions with human nature.

It is no use going into the details of his innumerable acts of material magnanimity that I witnessed, but I will recall only a few. As a man born in Usen and who belonged to one of the prominent secret cults in the place, he was an expert in esoteric incantations.

In 1948, a relation of his called Mr. Otote sent a message to my father that his wife Isere was in labor, and was at the point of death. My father asked me to light his lantern to follow him to Igun Street. At that time the hospital culture of the white man was not yet in vogue. My father was an expert in the pre-and postnatal care of pregnant women, knowledge which he said he acquired from his parents. We immediately left for Igun Street at about 2:30 am. When we got to Mr. Otote's house, the woman was virtually comatose. My father put his left knee down and began to repeat an incantation. By the time he repeated the stanza six times, the woman seemed to regain some consciousness. Subsequently a pair of male twin children emerged from the woman's womb, both already dead, but the woman was out of danger.

Òrúnmìlà has often told me that I should not try to convince converts to belong to him because it could needlessly interfere with the paths of their destiny. He only authorized me to write about him but not to preach about him, because when he comes into people's lives, it is for the purpose of making them happy, prosperous and to live longer. My father prepared Ifá for no less than one thousand men and women whose lives subsequently attained greater heights of fulfillment, including very prominent men in Benin.

He performed a few wonders some of which I would like to highlight in this book. In 1950, after his second wife temporarily left him, there was utter confusion in his house. One day, he had a disagreement with my mother over food money. He became so paranoid that he repeated the incantation for self-immolation and he lapsed into a coma and would have died but for the intervention of a visiting uncle, Chief Ironi from Usen, who succeeded in using the anti dotal incantation to revive him.

In 1949, one of his relations on the same street with him called Mr. Osifo, had gone raving mad. After stabbing a prominent woman and daughter of his neighbor, a meeting of the landlord of the street was held at the home of the Head Chief, Iyamu Eruogun on what to do about his mad cousin's menace. After the meeting dispersed, Mr. Osifo was waiting for the crowd in front of his house at No. 7 Edo College Road in Benin. As soon as he cited my father, he accused him of betraying him to non-relatives. As soon as he assailed my father, everyone around was astounded to see Mr. Osifo falling to the ground repeatedly until the seventh time, when he could not get up. It was my father who had to lift him up with his left hand, after which the man went inside his house. Three days later, he was bundled into an asylum by the government as a result of the stab wound he had inflicted on a woman called Aiyinomwan, in the Aro Hospital, where he died many years later.

In 1950, we were clearing the site of my present dwelling house behind my father's house in Benin, when his neighbor, who had been contesting the boundary with him; stealthily came behind my father's house in Benin, to use a machete on my father. No one noticed his action until his right hand holding the cutlass was transfixed in the air and when he started wailing with words "Mr .Odin, please help me, let my hand come down." The man learned to respect my father from that day until he died a few years later, in his mid forties and before retiring from the Public Service. The next illustration I'd like to make of the kind of man my father was, is what he did to get my eldest brother back to Benin after he had hibernated in Lagos with my father's only sister from 1947 to 1951, during which he never attended any school. In her characteristic altruism, my mother had been obsessed with the feeling that if my senior brother did not do well in life, I would have lots of problems. She subsequently went to an Augurer who told her what sacrifice to make before advising her husband to do something to bring his eldest son home.

One night, my father asked me to follow him to the front of the house with a lantern. When we got outside, he stripped in total nudity and began to repeat an incantation several times, adding in Benin language "If it was this genital that brought Oweonrisiede (my senior brother's name) to the world, he should set aside all else and hurriedly come home from wherever he was within the next seven days. Thereafter, he dressed up and we went in to sleep for the night. That was in 1951 when I was already in Class 4 in the secondary school. I was flabbergasted when I saw my senior brother three days later. That was when he subsequently resumed his education in Primary five, where he left off.

The next notable incident occurred in 1968 during the Nigerian civil war. His most senior Ifá son and next house neighbor, Chief Asemota Omoregie, the grand-duke of Iguosodin-nigbemaba, was ill and hospitalized. My father went on his push bicycle to visit the man. As he was coming out of the gates of the specialist hospital in Benin, a car hit him. While the military passengers of the car were looking for the victim of the accident, people were astounded to see him sitting, unscathed on the roof of the car. It was that event that made me buy his first secondhand car for him at a cost of one hundred and sixty pounds.

The last spectacular events of his life worthy of mention are the two incidents that made him die at age 87 instead of 92. An Indian astrologer had told me in New Delhi in 1971 that my father was going to die at age 92. This prediction was confirmed to me by Òrúnmìlà ten years later in 1981, when the wisdom divinity disclosed that I should be arranging for my father's burial at age 92, unless he shortened his life span by deliberate action.

The prediction manifested between 1989 and 1990. After I had a cardiovascular accident (stroke) in 1989 on my way home from a lecture tour of the United States, things began to happen. First his third wife was entranced into making an open confession, when she was esoterically insensated into mentioning the names of the demonic witches in our family. Out of pride, my father stopped her by putting a wand called "Odinmina eita" or "the dumb dreams but cannot narrate it." Thereafter, the woman, who had no bad intentions of her own because she was being used by the divinities and our ancestors to expose the evil doers in our family, did not say one more word. When we questioned my father later, he explained that it would injure the pride and name of the family if the world knew that there had been a spate of confessions in Chief Osague's house. It turned out later that the ancestors did not take kindly to my father's action because they wanted to expose the evil doers who were doing their utmost to extinguish the stars of the family.

The second factor that precipitated his premature death was his external determination not to allow any of his children to die before him. He thought that the stroke that afflicted me was going to terminate my life before him especially after one of his cousins, an Ifá priest in Ondo, died of stroke at the University of Benin teaching hospital on February 6, 1990. My father died the next day. When I realized that my father had a second reason for inviting death to terminate his life, I insisted and moments before he died, he called me alone and told me that apart from myself, another child of his was likely to die within three years and he did not wish to be alive to see it happen. His predictions came true in 1992, less than three years after his own death. That was the greatest father I knew about.

The Late Chief Thompson Ibie Odin
The Osague of Benin

IFISM
The Complete
Works of Òrúnmìlà

Volume Eight
The Odus of Irosun

```
 I
 I
 I
I I
I I
```

Chapter **1**

IROSUN-OGBE
IROSUN-GBAGBE LOJU
IROSUN-AKEREGBE

```
 I  I
 I  I
 I  II
 I  II
```

He Made Divination for Ugun And Elulu:

Shi juun ki o ba ri abore je. Adifa fun Ugun, abufun Elulu. Do not be greedy if you wish to prosper, was the name of the Awo who made divination for Ugun (Ugu in Bini) and Elulu (Erimohi in Bini))the two sons of Oloore when they were arranging to ascend the throne of their father. They were both advised to make sacrifice. Elulu was the senior of the two brothers and he was told at divination to make sacrifice with a he-goat, akara, eko, ground-nuts, fried corn, and palm fruits, and to set a trap on the shrine of Èsù to catch the head of the he-goat. Since he was the heir apparent, who had the first refusal option, he could not appreciate why it was necessary for him to make any sacrifice on account of what was his traditional entitle-ment. He refused to make the sacrifice. Ugun, the junior of the two brothers was also told to make the same sacrifice, adding a trumpet to the sacrifice. He made the sacrifice conscientiously.

After the burial of their father, the children had to mourn their father for fourteen days in separate secret conclaves, without having any food or drinks. Every morning, Èsù was feeding Ugun with the materials with which he had made sacrifice. On his part Elulu had nothing to eat and became very weak from hunger.

On the fourteenth day, Elulu was invited by the king makers to come to the palace for the crowning ceremony. He could scarcely walk. On his way however, he saw an attractive palm fruit by the side of the road. As he was traveling on horseback to the coronation site, he decided to reach for the palm fruit. Unknown to him, the palm fruit was the bait of a trap. As he stretched out himself to pick it up his neck was trapped. Try as he did to set himself free, he could not. The trap subsequently strangled him to death.

After waiting in vain to see Elulu, the kingmakers sent messengers to bring him for the coronation ceremony. They were surprised to see his horse without him. They decided to trail him to his house. On the way, however, they found him dead in a trap. When the messengers reported their findings to the kingmakers, they immediately sent for Ugun, who turned up without any delay. They told him about the unexpected death of his brother and told him that it was his turn to become the Oloore of Ore. He was eventually crowned and subsequently invited his diviner for thanksgiving feast at which he sang:

Amugun joye Oloore
Amado do wi ise.

When this Ifa appears as Uree at divination, the person should be advised to make sacrifice and to beware of greediness. He should forbid eating palm fruits and any red fruit. He should make sacrifice with cock and rabbit. The rabbit should be used for sacrifice to the elders of the night and deposited at the road junction near his house.

If it appears at Ayeo, the divinee should make sacrifice with a he-goat, palm fruits, akara, eko, ekuru and a trumpet, in order to achieve the upliftment coming his way and to avoid sudden death before the achievement.

He Made Divination for Olobaghun and Idanigbo:

Uroke Amerun jingini. Odifa fun Olobaghun, abufun Idanigbo.

Uroke with the pointed mouth, made divination for the Tortoise and Idanigbo when they were contesting for their father's chieftaincy title. They were advised to make sacrifice, but the Tortoise was in no mood to make any sacrifice. Idanigbo was advised to make sacrifice with he-goat and crushed yam (elo or obobo). He was told to sprinkle the crushed yam from his house to the coronation site. He did the sacrifice as he was advised.

The Ifa priest prepared the crushed yam with the iyerosun of the Odu and gave it to him to spray to the installation venue. When the two brothers left the following morning for the venue, the Tortoise asked Idabigbo why he was spraying crushed yam along the route and he replied that he knew what he was doing. When he could no longer resist the lure of the crushed yam, the Tortoise slowed down and began to feed on it. As he was eating the crushed yam, the Tortoise began to sing:

Oye Oye re o Idanigbo
Idanigbo ma de wo danu
Oye oye re o Idanigbo

He was virtually conceding the title to Idanigbo as he sang and ate the crushed yam along the route. Idanigbo arrived at the venue while there was no trace of the Tortoise. Idanigbo was eventually given the title.

If it appears as Ayeo at divination, the person should be told that he should forget about a position for which he is contesting. If it is Uree, he should be told to make sacrifice in order to succeed. If the contest is for a chieftaincy title or a position of authority, he should make sacrifice with a ram, a tortoise and crushed yam in order to succeed.

He Made Divination for Òrúnmìlà When He Was Surrounded By Enemies:

Ino jo oke se ti okun. Orun wo si abata. Adifa fun Òrúnmìlà baba mbe ni irangun ota.
Fire was extinguished by sea water. Heat was humored by the swamp.

These were the two Awos who made divination for Òrúnmìlà when he was surrounded by enemies. He was told to make sacrifice with a he-goat, cutlass, club, rabbit, and mud missile (ekpakpa in Yorùbá and udugbe in Bini). He made the sacrifice and his enemies began to die one after the other.

When it appears as Ayeo at divination, the person should be told that he or she has many enemies, but would overcome them if sacrifice was made. If it is Uree, he will obtain help from other people in whatever he is planning to do.

How Orunmila Solved The Problem of His Three Sworn Enemies:

Death, Water and Fire set out to attack Orunmila. Their identities and conspiracy were revealed to him in a morning divination. He then repeated the following poem three times:-

"I have not seen what you have contemplated except death; what is it that deprives one of one's belonging except, the river: I do not know what can take away without retribution except Fire. Orunmila however proclaimed that neither Death, Water nor Fire could take anything from him and get away with it. He gave a ram to his Ifa, who Olókun drove Death away. He also served; Èsù with he-goat, Olókun with pigeon, and Ògún with cock. Olókun stopped any threat to Orunmila from Water and Ògún checked the menace from Fire. He was then left alone in peace and tranquillity.

He Made Divination for Agbeni Maima:

Oshe ba ile ile, ofi she jana igi
Oshe iyale ile, ofi she oja I jokun gbo run
Adafa fun agbe-ni-ma-rima ti nshe oko Biogbe.

Agbeni maima was a divine priest who used to travel to the side of the sea for Awo practice. He was away from home for Awo practice most of the time. Whenever he was away, his wife Bioje missed him so much that she often contemplated leaving him. Her intentions were always revealed to her husband by a charm he carried with him.

Anytime he saw the sign that his wife was planning to leave, he would use his okpa-orere (osegan in Bini) to procure stomach trouble for her at home. Thereafter, she was singing in praise of her husband, who would subsequently return to make her well. As soon as she became well, he would travel out once more and the cycle would resume.

After three such experiences, Agbeni-maima got fed up with his wife's constant threat to leave. He decided on a fourth occasion to allow her to please herself. He allowed her to leave and she wandered into the world and no one ever saw her again. No one knew where she died or where she was buried.

If this odù appears for a woman at divination, she should be told not to leave her husband, lest she would suffer untold hardship. If it appears for a man, he should be advised to have a heart-to-heart talk with his wife because some evil force is urging her to leave him.

Made Divination for Ojiji:

He made divination for Ojiji when he was the chief diviner to the Olofin. Ojiji was responsible for making daily divination for Olofin, but before going to the Oba's palace, he often made divination for himself. His predictions invariably came true and Olofin reposed a whale of confidence in him.

At one morning divination for himself, he was required to serve Èsù with he-goat before going to the palace. Not wanting to spend his own money to buy the he-goat, he contemplated asking the Olofin to provide a he-goat for sacrifice, on getting to the palace.

When he got to the palace, he embarked on the day's divination, and predicted to the Olofin that it was going to be a good day, because three hunters would report to the palace with elephant, lion and tiger, and that 200 persons would arrive to pay homage to him and that Olofin would deliver at the Royal harem on that day. He vouched that if his predictions failed to materialize, he should be executed.

Up to midday on that day, nothing had happened. After the divination, Èsù asked for who did not make sacrifice by shouting "Agbo" to Ighoroko who replied "Afakan" and announced that Ojiji failed to make sacrifice before going to Olofin's palace. Èsù reacted by taking position at the main road leading to the town where he pegged two sticks on either side of the road and tied palm frond to them.

When the elephant hunter was coming to the palace, he was stopped by Èsù. When he explained that he was going to the palace to report that he had shot an elephant, Èsù told him that Olofin had escaped from the palace because war had broken out in the town. In a similar manner, Èsù who assumed the posture of an elder statesman, stopped, the lion and tiger hunters and the 200 homage carriers who were going to seek audience with the Olofin.

At dusk, Olofin sent for Ojiji to tell him that none of his predictions had come true. Olofin's pregnant wife went into labor, but Èsù stopped her. In consonance with the pledge he had given, Olofin ordered that Ojiji should be stoned to death. After he had been stoned for a long time, he fell to the ground and was presumed dead. Èsù also thought that Ojiji had died because he subsequently removed the palm frond from the road. First, Olofin's wife went into instant labor and delivered at the palace a baby boy. Next, all the hunters and homage payers, reported at the palace, albeit late in the evening.

When Olofin saw that all of Ojiji's predictions had belatedly come true, he rushed out of his chair to stop the stoning of Ojiji, but his foot struck the frame of the door, and blood began to flow from the injury to his foot. When he persuaded Ojiji to stand up, his feet could not support him. He was however still alive, but could only stand on his feet by being supported by another person. He subsequently became the shadow which does not stand up by itself.

When this Odu appears at Ugbodu, the person should serve; Ifa with two ducks and Èsù with he-goat. At divination, the person should be advised to serve Èsù with a he-goat in order to get on well in his job.

Made Divination for Lakangbo Before Becoming King:

Gun, ugun, omo elewu mofin ala,
Akala maigbo, omo elewe figo figo l'orun, ati
Agun fon ni iyanda, Awo ile ade pele.

These were the three Awos who made sacrifice for Lakangbo when he was contesting for the Olofin's throne. He was advised to make sacrifice with a ram and white cloth. He was also told to have his own Ifá. He made the sacrifice and Agunfon iyanda prepared Ifá for him. The sacrifice was made with the following incantation:

The rat makes sacrifice before entering his hole.
The fish makes sacrifice before entering the river.
Birds make sacrifice before flying freely in the air.
Animals make sacrifice before roaming the forest.

The seed makes sacrifice before entering the shells.
Human beings make sacrifice before entering their houses.
Just as you Lakangbo has made sacrifice before assuming kingship.
Long may you reign in peace and prosperity over the land of Ife.

When the king-makers eventually made divination on who was to become the next Olofin, the lot unanimously fell on Lakangbo because Èsù had meanwhile successfully lobbied all the king-makers on his behalf. The divination was done by two Awos called Opoye Lakodi and Omi adagba si yi fo. They were the Ifá priests who confirmed that it was the turn of Lakangbo to become king. When Lakangbo subsequently appeared at their auditorium, all the king-makers greeted him with KA-BI-YE-SI-O!

He was accordingly given plenty of wives and pages and became very prosperous. On the third anniversary of his coronation he invited his main diviner, Agunfon Iyanda and made a big feast in his honor.

When this ODu appears at divination, the person will be told that there is a big title in his family, or a higher position in his place of work which will fall to his turn if he makes sacrifice with a big ram and white cloth. He should arrange to have his own Ifá if he does not already have one. He should be told that Ifá will reward him bountifully if he serves him conscientiously.

Chapter **2**

IROSUN-OYEKU
IROSUN-ARIKU

```
 ||   |
 ||   |
 ||   ||
 ||   ||
```

The Divination He Made Before Leaving Heaven:

Kekere awo, pelu Agba awo. Awon mejeji l'ondifa fun Orunmila ni jo ti owa ye. A young Awo and an elderly Awo were the two diviners who made divination for Orunmila at the beginning of time. They advised him to serve his guardian angel with a guinea-fowl and to make sacrifice to enemies with three snails. He was to cover the mouth of the first snail with mud, the second one with salt, and to leave the third one as it is. The sacrifice was to be made to avoid trouble from enemies on earth. He did the sacrifice before leaving for the world.

The first divination he made on earth was for a pregnant woman. He advised her to wash her head with a he-goat on Èsù shrine in order to avoid having problems during delivery. She made the sacrifice and subsequently had a safe delivery.

Meanwhile, he was having problems from enemies, but on account of the precautionary sacrifice he made in heaven, they could not do anything to him. To live on earth, he was advised to pray to, and serve Èsù every day, and to give him whatever he asked for. He did as he was told and lived to a ripe old age, and outlived all his enemies.

When this Odu appears at Ugbodu or divination, the divinee should be advised to serve Èsù always because Èsù will help him/her to overcome his/her enemies.

He Made Divination for a Divine Priestess called Oye:

He made divination for Oye when she was anxious to have a child. The woman made the sacrifice recommended for her with a guinea-fowl to her head and a he-goat to Èsù. She became pregnant and subsequently gave birth to a male child who was named Ifamudewa.

Over time the divine priestess Oye was herself capable of giving medicine to pregnant woman for safe deliveries. On one occasion she gave medicine to two pregnant woman with the support of Orunmila to have safe deliveries. They both had male children, who were given Ikin (ude) and they were both named Ifamudewa.

One of the two woman was however very arrogant because she was a witch. After delivery, the witch woman paid no homage to Orunmila. She only made occasional visits to Oye who however told her not to be ungrateful to her benefactor, Irosun-Oyeku. Not long afterwards, her child became ill. When she went to Oye, she told her to go to Orunmila with a guinea-fowl, four snails, rat, fish and kola nuts, and that whatever medicine he gave to the child would make him well. She eventually went to Orunmila, with the materials, who made sacrifice for her. At divination, he told her that she was responsible for the child's sickness. He accused her of heartlessness, for attempting to kill a child she was so anxious to have The woman admitted the accusation and promised to released the child. He became well soon afterwards. Orunmila then sang a song.

> E ba mi dupe lowo Oye mo Oye.
> Oye mo wa shere, Oye ta ni no omo

Meaning:

> Thank Oye for me, Oye thank you,
> Oye the benevolent one that is, for helping to save her own child's life.

When this Ifa appears at Ugbodu, the person should immediately prepare Èsù with a he-goat and serve the new Ifa with a guinea-fowl, four snails, rat, fish and kola nuts because of his children. He should be advised to try always to be humble and to refrain from being arrogant. At divination, the person should serve Èsù with he-goat to avoid losing his rightful position to someone else. He should also serve his head with a guinea-fowl.

The Sacrifice for Undulating Fortunes:

> Ifa ni Ikalaye kpaye, Emina Mikalaye kpaye.
> Oni kaaso fun omo Ogun, ko tera ma ebo riru.
> Oun fo kalaye kpaye, Emina mo fo kalaye kpaye.
> Ifa ni ka so fun omo Uja, ko tera me ebo riru
> Orunmila oloun se kalaye kpaye, Emina fo kalaye kpaye.
> Oni ka so fun akakpo mi, ko te ra me bo riru.
> Orunmila oun so fun kalaye kpaye, Emina fo kalaye kpaye.
> Oni ka so fun omo orisa ko te ra mebo riru.

A situation in which one fortune arrives to substitute for an existing one instead of complementing it, is called alaye kpaye, such as losing a child as soon as another is born, or losing a wife after marrying a second one.

To stop the trend from recurring, Orunmila advised the children of Ogun, Uja, Òrìsà and his own children, to make sacrifice with he-goat, cock, scissors, black and white threads, in addition to the relevant leaves to be procured by the Ifa priest.

The he-goat is given to Èsù. The blood of the cock is used to grind the leaves, and marked round the wrists. The rest of the medicine is molded round the scissors and tied in place to be kept in the pocket always.

When Irosun Oyeku appears at divination, the person should be advised to make this special sacrifice to avoid replacing one fortune with another. If it comes out for a woman, she will be told to make the sacrifice to avoid the danger of not staying long with any husband. The same is true of a man.

Sacrifice for Pregnancy and Safe Delivery:

Mi ki 'rososun ta kele kulu. Emina miki 'rosun takele kulu.
Eyi to ta kele kkulu si ku omo eku omo eja, ati omo eni. Oyun
lo fi ni, omo lofi 'bi.

Irosun was told to transform the wombs of the rat, fish and a woman, in order to make them pregnant and hear children. They were advised to make the necessary sacrifice for pregnancy and safe delivery. The sacrifice was made with a cock and a hen.

If it appears at divination, the person should be told that he has a pregnant woman around him, who should be advised to make sacrifice in order to deliver safely.

Sacrifice for Warding Off The Danger of Death:

Orunmila ki Irosun ye ku, Emina ni ki Irosun ye ku.
Orunmila ni kini Irosun yi o fi ye ku.

Orunmila told Irosun to drive death away.
I also told Orunmila to drive death away.

Orunmila asked Irosun what was to be used to drive death away. Irosun replied that he did not know what to use for driving death away. Orunmila told Irosun to use rat, fish, akara, eko, rabbit, hen, cock, kola and a bottle of oil and guinea-fowl.

If it appears as Ayeo at divination, it means that death is on the person's trail, and that he or she should make sacrifice to ward off the danger. If it is Uree, make sacrifice with pigeon, akara and eko.

Another Sacrifice for Driving Death Away:

Orunmila said that people talk about one when one, is prosperous, marrying a new wife, having a child, becoming a chief, building another house, and when one dies.

He then advised that to keep death away, it requires sacrifice with a ewe (sheep or agutan).

Agutan mo ri borogi,
Ka kimi ku, Ma fi di'le,
Olorun ti'le Kun, a o ni ku si omode.
Agidi mogbon yin, Olorun ti ilekun.

I had to use the sheep for sacrifice,
To prevent my life from passing away.
I will use the sheep to appease the ground, and
Beseech God to lock the door against death.

We shall not die young. I stubbornly refused, and
begged God to seal up the path of death.

When it appears at divination, the person will be advised to make sacrifice to avoid death.

Chapter **3**

IROSUN-IWORI

```
II  I
 I  I
 I  II
II  II
```

The Divination He Made Before Leaving Heaven:

He was advised in heaven to offer sacrifice to a divinity which operates under cover of a curfew (Oro), with a cock, kola nuts and palm wine, and to serve Èsù with a he-goat. He did the sacrifices. The twin brothers Irosun and Iwori then came together to the world.

Meanwhile, Irosun plotted with fifteen witches of the night to eliminate Iwori. While sleeping one night, Iwori had a dream in which he saw an execution chamber. Not comprehending the significance of the dream, he decided to embark on divination. Ifá told him that he was about to be deceived, but that it would come to naught if he gave a he-goat to Èsù and serve his Ifa with a hen and dried rolled fish, he did.

Of the sixteen persons involved in the plot against Iwori, two died leaving fourteen of them. Subsequently, the Awos told him that it was his junior brother, who contrived the plot against him. He had one Osanyin (Osun-Oghirare in Bini) which was capable of making him see what was happening at the nocturnal meetings of witches. After serving it with a cock, crushed yam without oil mixed with ginger seeds, (ighere in Yorùbá and oziza in Bini), he was translated to the meeting of witches that night at which he saw the contrivances of the fourteen conspirators.

The witches however felt the presence of an intruder and organized a search. Iwori was subsequently caught and he was accused of spying. He however disappeared before they could do anything to him.

When he woke up in the morning, he consulted Ifa who advised him to invite Ifa priests to prepare leaves for him to have a bath. After having the bath, the conspirators, knowing that he had known their plans, went off his back and left him alone.

When the Ifa appears at divination, the person should be advised to makè sacrifice to Ifa with a hen and rolled fish and Èsù with a he-goat, in order to thwart the evil machinations of his junior brother against him. He should be told that his junior brother is a witch.

He made Divination for Akogun:

When Akogun, the military commander was going to war, he went to Irosun-Oyeku for divination. He was advised to make sacrifice with; he-goat to Èsù, dog to Ogun, and cock to his head, before leaving home. Since he could not imagine any force that could defy his invincible magic powers and physical strength, he did not bother to make the sacrifice. He subsequently left for the battle front accompanied by his wife. At the war front, he was victorious because it took him no time to subdue the enemies. When he was returning home in triumph, he came across a river where a python was having its bath. It is dangerous for anyone to see the python when having its bath. It has its bath by hooking its head to a tree on one side of the river, while tying its tail to a tree on the other side of the river. Thereafter, it begins to splash its body against the water and the resultant noise can be deafening.

When Akogun heard the deafening sound, he wondered what new battle was raging in front of him, because that was what the noise sounded like. He however asked his wife to go and see what was happening. When his wife saw the python, she ran back with the exclamation "Irosun wo Iwori wo" meaning, that her husband should come and see for himself, because what two pair of eyes see is more factual than what one pair of eyes sees. When he saw the python having its bath, he was annoyed that his wife invited him to see an ordinary boa constrictor, a snake. He wondered what a snake could do to a warrior who was used to doing battle with armed opponents.

As he was talking, the python felt the presence of intruders and rushed at them. As the snake made for him, he stretched out his leg towards it and it began to swallow it. The python had mauled him to the waist before he brought out his dagger to split its mouth to the point his legs had reached inside the stomach. He was surprised when he freed his legs to see that they were paralyzed. He could not walk home and had to be carried by his wife.

On getting home he decided that he could not continue to live as a cripple. He transfigured into Odole (Ivie-Ogun in Bini) which the blacksmiths use for knocking objects into the required shape. He had paid a high prize for his conceitedness and refusal to make sacrifice.

When the Ifa appears at Ugbodu, the person should immediately serve; Ogun with a dog, Èsù with a he-goat, his own head with a cock, and offer food (rabbit) to the elders of the night. At divination, the person should be told to serve; Ogun with a dog, and his head with a cock if a man or guinea fowl, if a woman.

He Made Divination for The People of Iwoye:

Kpomu sheghe, awo won lo'de Iwoye. Odifa fun won l'ode
Iwoye ni bi ti won t'in fi omi oju shu bere gbogbo ure.

He made divination for the people of Iwoye when they were longing for prosperity generally. The people had been suffering from want and deprivation when they decided to invite Kpomusheghe to make divination for them. He advised them to make sacrifice with 10 pigeons, 10 rats, 10 fish, 10 hens, 10 cocks, 10 cowries, 10 yards of cloth and a goat.

After making the sacrifice, all attributes of prosperity which had left the town began to return.

Following the return of prosperity, there was general rejoicing in the town and they began to sing in praise of Kpomusheghe in the following words:

> Kpomusheghe, awo Iwoye, gbogbo ure, aje, oyun.
> Kpelu omo ti de Iwoye, Okpomusheghe awo Iwoye.

When this Odu appears as Ayeo at divination for an individual, he should be told that he has no wife or if he has one, that she is proposing to leave him, that his wife is not settled. He should make sacrifice with cock, hen and pigeon. If it is Uree, he should serve his head with cock and pigeon.

Orunmila Advises The Divinee To Watch His or Her Steps:

> Orunmila ni ki Irosun wo Irin to ma rin.
> Ariwo urinrin ni ika fi kpomo eku, omo eja, omo eran,
> ati omo eniyan.

Orunmila warned Irosun to watch out his steps because it is the rat, fish, antelope, and goat that did not watch the moves they made in the morning, which became victims of death before the end of the day.

Orunmila advised akpetebi to watch her steps because it is the person who failed to mind his steps in the morning that was killed by death before the end of the day. He however advised caution and sacrifice with a he-goat to Èsù adding cutlass and cudgel.

If this Odu appears at divination, the person should be told to watch his movements in order to avoid sudden death, or to avoid coming across danger that could lead to death. In addition to looking before leaping, he should also make sacrifice.

He Was Asking To Make Sacrifice at His Ancestral Home:

Irosun-Iwori was born at Iwoye but he spent his working life at Ife. When his Ifa practice was waning, he went to his Ifa priest called Otita mi omu di'rebe rebe for divination. He was told to return to his home base at Iwoye and to buy a goat for sacrifice. He was advised to invite all available Awos at Iwoye to prepare leaves including the leaves used for wrapping eko and ekuru (ebieba in Bini) to wash his Ikin and to bath with it thereafter.

He did as he was advised and his business became more rewarding and prolific when he returned to Ife. At the height of his prosperity, he invited his Awo for a feast where he sang:

> Otita mi omu da irebe rebe,
> Odafuun Orunmila je sa lo so'de Iwoye.
> Ifa we mi sa-o-ose Iwoye,
> Are da ra o ose Iwoye,
> Ifa we mi da o ose Iwoye,
> Awe dara o ose Iwoye.

He was singing in praise of the efficacy of the sacrifice made for him by his diviner and the Awos of Iwoye.

When the Odu appears at divination, the person should be told to have his own Ifa, but if he already has one, he should have it washed with a goat and the appropriate leaves at the place where the Ifa was prepared for him, in order to prosper.

Aweda Divined for The People Of Iwoye:

Aweda was the Awo who made divination for the people of Iwoye when they were suffering from disease called ogbogbo in Yorùbá, which they were ashamed to disclose. They were advised to make sacrifice with plenty of black soap, plenty of ginger seeds, rat (eku oloya). Aweda prepared the soap for them to bath with in the river. They all recovered from the sickness after having their bath in the river. There was general rejoicing and they began to dance and sing in praise of Aweda in the following words:

Aweda awo Iwoye, difa fun won l'ode Iwoye,
Aweda kpele, awo Iwoye Ifa.
Iwo ni yi o we mi da,
Awo Iwoye Aweda,
Awo Iwoye.

When it appears at divination the person should be told that a pregnant woman is close to him. The Ifa priest should prepare leaves for her to bath, and when the child is born, he or she should be named Ifawemida.

Chapter **4**

IROSUN - IDI

```
 |   |
 ||  |
 ||  ||
 |   ||
```

The Divination Made for Him Before Leaving Heaven:

One wakes up after sleeping, and
Better to tell a child about salvation
Rather than death, at divination.

These were the Awos who made divination for Irosun-Idi when he was coming to the world. He was told to make sacrifice because his success was going to provoke enemies around him on earth. He was required to serve Èsù with a he-goat. He became a practicing Ifa priest and a very effective one at that. He became so prosperous that his success evoked enmity among his relations and other diviners. As he began to experience difficulties procured for him by his enemies, he went for divination. He was told to make sacrifice with a he-goat to Èsù, who eventually helped him to checkmate the evil plans of his enemies.

He Made Divination for The Cat, Rat and Fish:

The cat, the rat and the fish went to him for divination. He told the cat to make sacrifice to avoid carrying the yoke of someone else's problem. He was told to make sacrifice to Èsù, his head and his guardian angel. He served his head and guardian angel, but failed to serve Èsù.

He also advised the rat to make similar sacrifices but he failed to make any. Meanwhile, the rat approached the cat to help him to catch the fish from the river. The cat replied that he did not know how to swim. The cat however decided to have a try when the rat promised to give him a fat meat if he succeeded in catching the fish for him.

The fish also went to Orunmila for divination, and he was told that enemies were plotting against him. Orunmila told the fish to make sacrifice with okra, soap and a hen. He quickly made the sacrifice. Orunmila added ewe tete, irorowo, and odondon to the okra to prepare soap for him to bath with. Thereafter, the fish took his abode in the water, where his body became slimy and slippery.

When the cat eventually went in search of the fish in the river, he met him dancing. The cat went on the attack, but the okra on the fish's body made it impossible for the cat to get hold of him. The fish then swam into the depth of the river and into safety from the threat posed by the cat, who returned home, disgusted. Before coming out of the water, the cat had drank plenty of water. It took him time to get rid of the water from his stomach. Thereafter, he went to the rat to demand the meat he promised to give him. He in fact demanded a goat to thank his head for not losing his life in the river.

On his part, the rat argued that since the cat did not succeed in coming with the fish, he was not entitled to demand an wager. The cat then attacked and killed the rat while the children ran away. It was from then on that the cat began to kill rat for food, because of the sacrifice he refused to make.

When this Odu appears at Ugbodu, the special sacrifice (ono-Ifa or odiha which was prepared for the fish should be made for the person to protect him form powerful enemies. If it appears at divination, the person should serve; Èsù with he-goat, his head with a cock, and Ifa with a hen, to avoid yoking someone else's problem.

He Made Divination for Onijama Akoko:

Bi aye ba ye won ton, iwa ibaje niwon uhi. Odifa fun Onijama
Akoko ti yio fi obinrin re mo oro.

At the height of prosperity, some people resort to base moral depravity. That was the name of the Awo who made divination for Onijama-akoko, a strong Ifa priest who loved his wife so much that there was no secret he could not disclose to her. In fact he prepared the wife to become diabolically and esoterically as strong as himself. Both himself and his wife could transfigure into both organic and inorganic substances.

As soon as the wife realized that there was nothing the husband could do which she could not do, she became conceited and contemptuous. Whenever he stretched out his hands to his wife, she would rain four insults on him. If he turned into a tiger, she would turn into a gorilla. The husband soon became totally incapable of doing anything to curb the insubordination of the wife.

Meanwhile, the Orò divinity was infuriated by the rudeness of Onijama's wife. That was the only cult to which Onijama-akoko could not initiate his wife, because it is forbidden for women to know the secret. In anger, the Oro divinity came out of the forest one night to kill Onijama-akoko's wife.

At divination for a woman, she will be advised to beware of behaving contemptuously towards her husband lest, she would die a sudden death, without prior sickness. For a man, he should be told that he is over-loving his wife by letting her into all his secrets, and that by so doing, he could be goading the woman to her death.

He Made Divination for Jika-Jiku Who Could Revive The Dead:

Simi titi, awo Simi Titi. Simi rere, awo simi rere.
Adafa fun Jika-Jiku ti'nshe ore akala.

Escort me far and escort me up to the point I choose, were the two Awos who made divination for Jika Jiku who specialized in restoring life to the dead, and who was friendly with a woman called Akala. Whenever anyone died, the relation raced to Jika-Jiku to restore their lives. He used to apply one medicine given to him by his fay colleagues in heaven. He was himself a fay. He often charged a lot of money for using the medicine to revive the dead. He used to apply the medicine to the head and chest of the deceased after which they would jump up after regaining life. He became very rich in the process and no one was going to heaven anymore.

Meanwhile, his colleagues began to wonder how he got that kind of medicine. Eventually, Akala, a very attractive woman decided to marry Jika-Jiku in order to find out the secret. She went to his house to profess love to him for reviving her relation to life. He agreed to marry her and she began to live with him right away. Any time he was invited to assist in reviving the dead, she often accompanied him. She became so familiar with his secrets that nothing was any more hidden from her.

Having discovered the secret of the medicine, Akala embarked on a program for stealing the container. One day, Jika-Jiku invited Akala to accompany him to the farm but she declined to go. As soon as he left for the farm, Akala collected all his instruments and left the house.

Meanwhile, Jika-Jiku was invited from the farm when someone died. He quickly returned to the house but when he asked for Akala, she was nowhere to be found. Thinking that his instruments were still in the bag, he collected the bag and followed the people who came to seek his assistance. When he got to the home of the dead person, he searched in vain for the container of the medicine in his bag. He ran home to look for it and for Akala, to no avail. He did not even know how to look for Akala because he had never bothered to know from where she came. That was a signal that he had finished his work on earth and that his time was up for returning to heaven. Without any sickness and without taking his own life, he died before the following morning.

It will be recalled that at divination, he had been advised against falling in love with a woman, without knowing her home, and to give a he-goat to Èsù in case he met such a woman. He did not perform the sacrifice and the magic of Akala had totally beclouded his vision.

When this Odu appears at divination for a man he should be warned to make sacrifice against a woman who would offer to marry him. He should not let her into his secrets because she would outwit and cheat him. If it appears for a woman, she should be advised not to double-cross any man.

Divined for Awele Who Dispensed Death With Her Genitals:

Simi titi, awo simi titi. Simi rere, awo simi rere.
Ako le simi titi ka simi de le eni. Adifa fun Awele omo oni di oringe le to ma fi obo ko jogbon sile l'ari she oko. Obo Awele ki je eku, ki je eja. Odidi eni l'onje.

No one escorts a visitor right up to his house, was the name of the Awo who made divination for Awele advising her to beware of how she used her genitals, to avoid killing with it. Her vulva neither fed on rats nor fishes. Its staple food was human beings. She was advised to make sacrifice to avoid killing people with her genitals, but she refused to do it.

Meanwhile, two lovers were concurrently befriending her. One lover was however physically stronger than the other, but the weaker one was, more handsome and head and shoulder more attractive. Awele visibly preferred the more good-looking suitor. The physically stronger man had courted Awele for a long time but she did not conceal her preference. Thinking that what stood between him and Awele was her more handsome admirer, he contrived a plan to get rid of him.

One day, he sharpened his machete and lay in ambush against the young man. After spending the night with Awele, the more handsome man was on his way home when he was attacked and murdered by the rejected suitor. It was that incident that earned Awele the nickname of the woman whose genitals feed on human beings.

When this Odu appears at divination for a woman, she should be advised to make sacrifice so that two men might not engage in fatal competition for her hand. She should make sacrifice with hen, cock, rabbit, rat, fish, akara and eko. If it appears for a man, he should be advised to make sacrifice with a he-goat and a cutlass to avoid losing his life on account of a woman.

He Made Divination for Sànkpàná, The Epidemics Divinity:

He made divination for Sànkpàná when he was invited by the Oba and people of Ikinmi to come and assist in putting the affairs of the town, right. He was advised to make sacrifice with a he-goat to Èsù, and a cock to his head, before going. When he however looked at the strong magical charms inside his bag, he concluded that no obstacle could disrupt his journey. He decided not to make any sacrifice. He then left for Ikinmi.

When Èsù was told that Sankpana refused to perform the prescribed sacrifice, the evil divinity vowed that he would never get to Ikinmi. Instantaneously, Èsù transfigured into a woman who had been attacked with a machete, which severed one of her breasts with blood gushing out. When she met Sankpana, she asked where he was going and he replied that he was heading for Ikinmi. The woman warned him not to go to Ikinmi because a vicious battle was raging in the place and it was as a result of the war the she injured her breast.

Sankpana however brought out his magic mirror from his bag, with which he telescoped into Ikinmi and saw that the people were waiting for him. He could not reconcile the reading from his mirror with the injured woman's story. He decided to ignore the woman and to continue on his journey.

He subsequently met a man with a severed hand and blood streaming out of his body. Èsù was at his game once more. When the man told Sankpana not to proceed on his journey to Ikinmi because of the battle raging in the town, he looked again at his mirror which disclosed that preparation for his reception was well advanced. Once again Sankpana ignored the man and proceeded on his journey. Not long afterwards, he met two hefty men running in fright. He subsequently heard a gunshot which hit one of the two men, who fell down, dead. The second surviving man told Sankpana that the Oba of Ikinmi had been killed. Thereafter, Sankpana was convinced that he could no longer rely on his magic mirror. He decided to sit down and wait. He did not enter Ikinmi until late in the night.

At the time of his arrival, the Oba was already annoyed for being kept waiting for so long, because the food and drinks prepared for his reception had all gone sour. When he narrated what kept him waiting on the way, the Oba told him that his story was too farfetched to be credible. He in turn became annoyed for being regarded as a liar and decided to return home at once.

When this Ifa appears at Ugbodu, the person should immediately prepare his Èsù with a he-goat to avoid doing an unappreciated favor. A chicken would be tied to the Èsù shrine to cry to death. At divination, the person should serve; Èsù with a he-goat, and Ogun with a cock in order to be successful in a task he is about to undertake.

Sacrifice for Alleviating Difficulties:

When this Odu appears at divination, the person should be told that he is having problems, but that with sacrifice, the problems would be resolved. The sacrifice should be made with a tortoise, white chalk and camwood, (osun in Yorùbá and umen in Bini), because the chalk does not experience misfortune in Benin, just as the camwood does not see misfortune in Oyo and Ekiti. Ajanigboro-so-lokute made divination for difficulties:

Ajanigboro-so-lokute was the Awo who made divination for Orunmila and the other divinities when they were going to have a spear-throwing contest (okpa-orere or osogan) with Death. They were advised to make sacrifice with rabbit.

It was only Orunmila who made the sacrifice. When the time for the contest came, all of them threw their spears on stony ground and they could not stand or stick to the ground. When it was the turn of Orunmila to throw his spear, Èsù caused a rabbit to escape from the ground, which gave him the indication that, it was the only point at which his spear could stick to the ground and stand erect. He threw his spear into the rabbit's hole and it stuck firmly to the ground. Death was not happy to see that Orunmila succeeded in the contest. Asked why he decided to contest with Death, Orunmila explained the following song:

Ajanigboro-so-kute ni odifa fun oun Orunmila,
Oni oun gbo riru ebo, oun ru,
Oun si gbo eru tu kesu, oun tu,
Oni bi iku ba so okute,
Emi yio ba so kute.
Bi Oba so kute, emi yio ba so kute,
Ajanigboro so kute.

He explained that he embarked on the contest because he went for divination to Ajanigboro-so-kute and he did the prescribed sacrifice, and since sacrifice manifests unfailingly for those who make it, that is the secret of his audacity and success.

When it appears at divination, the person will be told that temptation or a strong test is imminent. He should therefore make sacrifice with a rabbit to avoid or triumph in it.

Chapter **5**

IROSUN-OBARA
IROSUN-EGA

```
 I  I
II  I
II II
II II
```

Made Divination for Ega, The Fruit-Bearing Tree:

Okpe tiri Eluju, awo ega, Odifa fun te ni ti'nshe yeye ega. Okpe luju was the diviner who made sacrifice for Ega when she was anxious to have children. She was told to make sacrifice with all the crops in the farm. She was told to add her wearing apparel to the sacrifice so that human beings may not destroy her or her children after producing them. She made the sacrifice and had many children at the same time.

After having her children, she went back to the Awo, Okpe Eluju, to demand the return of her wearing apparel. After returning it to her, Èsù clad her children with the various colors of the apparel. Èsù also went to human beings to tell them that the children (fruits) of Ega were dainty for eating. In consequence, she lost all her children to humanity. The Yorùbá name for ega is kaare, which refers to all edible fruit bearing plants.

Made Divination for Adaba To Call Off The Bluff of The Tortoise:

Ogbe kpu le'yin ori. Eje suuru leyin orun. Adafa fun Adaba.
On losi awoju egbe re. Ebo ni ko ru, tori ki a ma she asheju.

A person matcheted on the occiput will spill blood on the neck, was the name of the Awo who made divination for the bird called Adaba when he overreached himself with greed. He was advised to make sacrifice to avoid disgrace and embarrassment. He was told to make sacrifice with rat, fish, cock, akara, eko and palm wine. He did not do the sacrifice.

He had developed the habit of wearing a wooden cutlass in a case which he tied round his waist whenever he attended the meetings of all the birds. He used to browbeat other birds by threatening to pull his cutlass from its case and he invariably succeeded in using that ploy to convince the others into allowing him to drink more than his fair share of the available wine. When his colleagues became disgusted with his churlish behavior, they went for divination to find out what to do to call off his bluster.

At divination, they were advised to give a he-goat to Èsù and they did the sacrifice without any delay. After the sacrifice the Awo gave them the Iyerosun to put in his drink the next time Adaba threatened them with his machete case. He advised them to give him enough drink until he fell asleep, after which they were to take a close look at his bogey weapon.

At the next meeting, after his customary threat, they allowed him to drink until he became thoroughly drunk and fell asleep. As soon as he fell asleep, the others brought out his much vaunted weapon, only to discover that the case contained a wooden cutlass. They returned the wooden cutlass in the case and decided to wait for the first chance to puncture his sham.

At the next meeting, the other birds began drinking without waiting for him. When he arrived at the meeting to see that others had started drinking, he challenged them to surrender all the remaining drinks to him. The others uncharacteristically reacted by telling him that he was talking nonsense and that he should do his worst if he was not going to be satisfied with his fair share of the drinks. When he threatened to bring out his cutlass, the others challenged him to bring it out and use it. He was astounded. That was the end of his bluster, having been thoroughly disgraced.

When this Odu appears at divination, the person should be advised to make sacrifice to avoid disgracing himself at a meeting he is going to attend.

He will be told that there is one person he is afraid of, who scares him whenever he speaks. If the indication is Uree, he should be advised to stop dreading the person because he cannot do anything to him. If it is Ayeo, he should be advised to make sacrifice in order to call off the man's braggadocio. The bogey man is a witch. He should make sacrifice with cock and cutlass. The Ifa priest will prepare the cutlass with the appropriate leaves and give it to the divinee to be keeping under his pillow. If the divinee is a woman, she will be told that she is often scared when a woman who is not very tall talks at their meeting. If it is Uree, she will be advised to stop fearing the smallish woman because although she is a witch, she cannot do anything to harm her.

Another Variation: He Made Divination for The Tortoise and the Weaver Bird:

The tortoise was in the habit of threatening people with a disused cutlass kept in a case and worn round his waist. Being a lazy drone, instead of working for his own upkeep, he used to move from house to house with his cutlass strapped to his waist to blackmail people into giving him food.

One day, he met the weaver birds (eye ega in Yorùbá and akha in Bini) holding a meeting, at which they were drinking palm wine. When he got to the meeting, he threatened to pull out his encased cutlass if the birds failed to give him a drink. Out of fear, they quickly served him with palm wine. Thereafter, he made it a habit to be showing up at the weekly meetings of the weaver birds to procure drinks under false pretenses.

When the weaver birds did not know what to do with him, they trooped to Irosun-Ega for divination, at which he told them to make sacrifice with a he-goat to Èsù. After making sacrifice, Irosun Ega told them what to do at the next meeting. They were advised to conceal themselves from view at the next meeting, save for one of them who was to challenge the tortoise to a drinking contest in seven days time.

At a subsequent meeting all the other weaver birds (they all look alike) hid themselves in an inner room, and only one of them was present at the conference chamber. The lone weaver bird challenged the tortoise to a drinking contest in seven days time if he knew he could drink. He readily accepted the challenge.

On the seventh day, all the other weaver birds again concealed themselves in the inner room leaving one of them ostensibly to undertake the contest with the tortoise. The tortoise told the bird to serve himself and him, the tortoise. As soon as the bird had his drink he excused himself to urinate in the toilet. He was immediately relieved by another bird and the relay continued in such a manner that each weaver bird only drank once. The tortoise with all his witticism could not discover how he was being outmaneuvered by the weaver birds. As the birds were doing their drinking relay, the tortoise was getting drunk.

In his state of delirium, he pulled out his disused cutlass from the case to demonstrate that it was harmless. The birds got together to have him thoroughly beaten and expelled with a warning never to bother them again.

When this Ifa appears at Ugbodu, the person should be advised never to drink in public places. He should serve Èsù with he-goat and to be circumspect at meetings. He should avoid the tendency to become greedy in order to live long in honor and respect. At divination, the person should be advised not to drink any alcohol for seven days. He should serve Ogun with palm wine and roasted yam because people are plotting to undo him with wine. He should also beware of meetings.

The Divination He Made Before Leaving Heaven:

Obara bale ra Ogun, Ale oun eba ira, were the two Awos who made divination for Irosun-Obara when he was coming from heaven. He was told to wash his head on the ground with two eggs and two snails, and to serve Èsù with he-goat, and his guardian angel with guinea-fowl. He did all the sacrifices to obviate the risk of having paranoia on earth.

Nevertheless, he became very erratic when he got to the world. One night his guardian angel advised him to repeat the sacrifices he made in heaven. He did it without delay. He washed his head on the ground with two eggs and two snails mashed with ewe irorowo and other soft Ifa leaves. Thereafter, his head became cool and he began to behave more humanely. He subse-quently became a famous and prosperous Ifa priest in the town of Ega.

When the Oloja of Ega heard about his fame, he sent for him. His proficiency earned him the role of the chief diviner to the Oloja of Ega. The Oloja had a long standing illness which his traditional Babalawos and physicians could not cure. When Irosun-Obara got to the palace, he told the Oloja after divination that he had an expensive gown which he inherited from his father. He told the Oloja that the garment had been spoilt by the elders of the night and that if he surrendered it to Èsù with a he-goat, he would become well. The Oloja quickly made the sacrifice and he became well. That is how Irosun-Ega became the Chief Royal Diviner of the Oloja of Ega

He Made Divination for Alaakpa When He Lived in The Midst of Witches:

Alaakpa had several problems caused by witches who were daily sleeping and waking up with him. He later invited Orunmila for divination and he was advised to make sacrifice with a frog, a wooden image (omolangidi in Yorùbá) bitter leaves, sasswood (obo in Yorùbá and oziya in Bini). He made the sacrifice, and he was told to be repeating the following incantation every night, on the ayajo prepared for him.

No one ever dares to swallow the emissions of the electric tree.
No witch can survive an attack from sasswood or Obo.
No witch eats bitter leaf. No witch can kill a wooden image.
Dogs forbid to eat frogs.

Thereafter, all the witches ran away from him one after the other and he finally had peace and tranquillity.

When this Odu appears at divination, the person will be told that he is surrounded by witches. He should look for an Ifa priest to prepare a similar protective device (Ayajo) for him and he will be rid of them.

Chapter **6**

IROSUN-OKONRON
IROSUN-AKARA

```
II   I
II   I
II   II
I    II
```

Divination Made for Him Before Leaving Heaven:

Moyen oru ko geere le. Moyin faale geere le.
Abinu ooni ara moobo yen. Awon meteta lo'ndifa fun
Orunmila nijo t'on ko le orun si wa kole aye.

Name sakes never kill each other. There is gain from the ground. One's enemy does not wish one to survive trial by ordeal. These were the three Awos who made divina tion for Orunmila when he was coming to the world. He was advised to make sacrifice because he was going to experience a lot of enmity in the process of his Ifa practice. He was told to serve; his head with a guinea-fowl, his Ifa with a goat, his guardian angel with white cloth, chalk and a basket of pigeons and Èsù with he-goat, broken or half calabash and crushed yam (Elo or obobo). He did all the sacrifices and obtained God's blessing before leaving for the world.

On getting to the world, he turned out to be an Ifa priest and became famous for not prescribing elaborate materials for sacrifices. He hardly ever prescribed sacrifice with a goat. He was specialized in making akpako or Ebo sacrifice with easily affordable materials. His modest and moderate approach to sacrifice however earned him the displeasure of the more elderly Ifa priests, who saw sacrifice as a means of earning a living on suffering humanity. They soon accused him of being a witch because it was generally believed that only priests who were witches were privileged to prescribe moderate sacrifices. For instance, it is believed that an Awo who is not a witch must in his own interest, recommend sacrifice with a goat before he can attempt to save a victim of witchcraft from the elders of the night.

When he however denied being a witch, he was ordered to go for trial by ordeal (that is to drink the concoction based on sasswood (obo in Yorùbá and iyin in Bini). Meanwhile, he went for divination and he was told to serve Èsù with he-goat, the meat of antelope and a stick. He did the sacrifice before going for the trial by ordeal. As if the rigors of a trial by ordeal was not hazardous enough, his enemies also suborned assassins to lay in ambush to kill him in the event of his surviving the trial by ordeal.

He drank the concoction of the ordeal and nothing happened to him. After vomiting the sasswood, he was given the white chalk of innocence and told to return home in triumph. As he was walking home, just before he reached the spot where his prospective assassins lay in ambush, Èsù released a live antelope from their midst and the ambuscades abandoned their main objective and pursued the antelope, which of course, they could not kill. As they were blaming one another for allowing the antelope to escape, a fight ensued. After fighting and injuring themselves, they were all arrested and arraigned before the Oba for disturbing the peace. By the time they were released from the Oba's palace, Orunmila was already safely back in his house.

Even then, as soon as they left the palace, they still went to his house and ordered him to chant the song of trial by ordeal, as proof of his survival. He told them that he knew no such song, but sang in praise of the Awo who made divination for him. After his triumph over the enemies, each of them began to profess allegiance to him.

He Made Divination for Senifiran:

Irosun Kain Kain, babalawo Seni firan. Odifa fun Senifiran.

He made divination for Senifiran advising him to make sacrifice so that one death in his family is not followed by several others. He was told to make sacrifice with an ewe (female sheep), and a duck. He made the sacrifice and death did not strike at the family.

When the Ifa appears at divination, the person will be advised not to get involved in any task or engagement requiring collective or group effort. If the divination is for a sick person, his people should be advised to make sacrifice because if he is allowed to die, many others will follow him to heaven. If in spite of the sacrifice, the person still dies, the fowl that has no feather ((in Yorùbá and okpikipi in Bini) will be used to prepare the medicine to be buried with his corpse in the grave, to stop the dead person from dragging others along with him.

If the divination appears for a woman who is desperately looking for a child, she will be told to marry an Ifa man because she is the wife of Orunmila. She will first give birth to a male child.

He Made Divination for Toibi When She Was Anxious To Have a Child:

Esunsun te kokoko dina, Onreti akponda kan kan. Adifa fun Toibi t'onfi omi oju shu bere omo turuutu. Esusun grass blocked the passage way in the bush in anticipation of the man with a very sharp machete. That was the name of the Awo who made divination for Toibi whose eyes had swollen red from crying for not having a child. She was advised to make sacrifice with a hen, 4 snails, and a pigeon. She made the sacrifice after which she left her husband to marry an Ifa priest. She became pregnant the following month and gave birth to a male child, followed in quick succession by four other children.

If the odù appears at divination for a man, he should be told, that he has problems with marrying a wife. He should arrange to have his own Ifa after which he would come across a woman who has not had a child before.

When it appears for a woman, she will be told that she is desperate to have a child. She should go and marry a man having his own Ifa subject to confirmation by another divination.

Before the Ifa man marries her, he will be advised to serve his Ifa with a goat. Alternatively, if she is already married, she will be advised to persuade her husband to arrange to have his own Ifa.

If the woman has no problem of childlessness, she will be told to try to identify a female relation who is crying to have a child, and advise her to marry an Ifa man because her children are with Orunmila.

He Made Divination for Agufanmiyangan Who Discarded His Ifa:

Ada-ni she awo eba orun. Adide ni shawo isale ile. Adifa fun
Agufanmiyangan to fi Ifa re si'le t'onlo ro oko.

The big bat (owo in Bini and adani in Yorùbá) is the Awo on the approach road to heaven. The small bat (eguen in Bini and adide in Yorùbá) is the Awo on earth. These were the two Awos who made divination for Agufanmiyangan who abandoned Ifa practice to take to farming, because he complained that Ifism could not bring him prosperity. His poverty became even more abject after he became a farmer. That was when he decided to go for divination to the two Ifa priests. They asked him whether he did not know that many of the beneficiaries of his Ifa practice had become prosperous. They admonished him for lacking the patience to wait for the dawn of his days of prosperity. The Ifa priests sang Ifa songs to embarrass him. Eventually, he gave up farming and returned to Ifa practice after begging Ifa with a hen and kola nuts to forgive him. He subsequently became very prosperous.

When it appears at divination for a man, he will be advised to hurriedly have his own Ifa, if he does not already have one. For a man with Ifa, he should be told to learn how to understand Ifa. For and Ifa priest, he should be advised to give up whatever work he is doing on the sideline and to concentrate fully on Ifa practice, because he is falling out of line. For a woman, she will be advised to marry an Ifa man if not married, or to persuade her husband to have his own Ifa, if already married. If the woman is past childbearing age (post-menopause) she should be advised to learn how to use cowries for divination, and be practicing it for a living.

He Made Divination for The Garrulous Seer:

He made divination for a talkative Awo called Tabita who was fond of claiming to be capable of knowing and seeing what was clearly beyond his capabilities, thus often finding himself fishing in troubled waters.

On one occasion he went to the market to declare that he could tell what and who killed the Oba's son who had just died, when in fact, he had no esoteric or psychic powers whatsoever. He promised to reveal to the Oba who and what was responsible for the death of the son on the next market day.

On the next market day, he went to the palace, but could not reveal who and what was responsible for the death of the prince. He however proposed that a bunch of palm fruits should be provided and suspended on a fork stick, and that by the time the fruits started dropping from the bunch, the culprit would die. After a period of fourteen days the palm fruits began to drop to the ground, but nothing happened.

When he was subsequently invited to explain the failure of his prediction and experiment, he lied that an elderly woman, who was one of the pillars behind the Oba was responsible for the death of the Oba's son and that she should be executed. The Oba unwittingly believed him and ordered the woman to be arrested for execution.

The following morning a flock of vultures descended on the courtyard of the palace. The Oba immediately invited his traditional diviners to find out the significance of the visiting vultures. After divination, they disclosed that they came to protest the condemnation of the innocent old woman, because vultures do no allow elders to be wrongly treated. The Oba immediately rescinded his earlier order and compensated the old woman for being wrongly accused and detained. The Oba then gave orders for the arrest and trial of Tabita for operating under false pretenses. Before the royal police got to his house, he escaped from the town never to return.

When this Ifa appears at Ugbodu, the person should be advised to beware of garrulousness. He should in any case make sacrifice so that the words from his mouth do not force him out of his abode or place of work. He should serve Ifa with a white goat within three months of going into Ugbodu. Thereafter, he should serve Ifa with a crocodile to avoid creating trouble for himself in his town. He should also serve Ogun and Uja each with a cock. At divination, the person should serve his head, Ogun and Uja with a cock each, praying not to get into trouble through the words of his mouth.

Sacrifice for Avoiding War or General Turmoil:

Orunmila declared that there was victory when;
Olota conquered Benin and occupied it;
Rin-Rin conquered Owo and occupied it;
Pepe conquered Asan and occupied it;
Orobojegi conquered Otun-moba and occupied it;
Ibebe conquered Akaka in Oyo and occupied it;
Erumole ajugotun and Erumole ajugosi captured Ibodo and
occupied it; while
He Orunmila overran heaven and remains there.

Orunmila therefore declared that if this odù appears at divination as Ayeo, and it portends trouble (or ija) the person will be told that a war is imminent and that he should make sacrifice with a he-goat to escape the dangers posed by it.

Chapter **7**

IROSUN-OWANRIN

```
II    I
II    I
I    II
I    II
```

He Made Divination for Orunmila When He Was Ostracized:

Owan gogogo bi atunishe. Okpo kpikpo oni ibaje.
Oro to obaje eni fifo, ake je je je lo bi.
Adafa fun Orunmila ni ojo ti teku teja ati eye tiwon
niwon o ba she mo. Ebo ni ko ru.

It was as rare as the scarcity of getting anyone who willingly
agrees to help others to prosper.
It was common as the abundance of people who disrupt
the fortunes of others.
It is better to be silent on a matter that is not easy to mention.

These were the Awos who made divination for Orunmila when the species of rats, fishes and birds collectively resolved to ostracize him and hold him at arms length. He was advised to make sacrifice with a he-goat, cutlass, eko and akara. He made the sacrifice, after which Esu told him to be using rats and fishes to serve his Ifa and to be feeding his children on the meat of birds.

When it appears at divination, the person will be advised to make sacrifice because three of his/her friends will turn against him or her. If it appears as Ayeo, the person should be told to avoid those friends once he or she identifies them. If it is Uree, they will surely stage a comeback.

He Made Divination for Ugun-Ogege:

Onaja, Onako, adafa fun Ugun Ogege. Ara lo'de on losha
wo fun won ni ilode.

They made divination for Ugun-Ogege when he was going to practice Awo art for the people of Ilode. On getting to Ilode, he lodged with a man who lived in a wretched house. Nobody took notice of Ugun on account of his ugly and unimpressive personality. Three days after his arrival, he went out and sat down at a place where people were gathered. While sitting and watching the events going on, he eavesdropped into a conversation between two women who were concluding arrangements to leave their husbands on grounds of childlessness.

He reacted by inviting them to his lodging after reassuring them that there was a better option than abandoning their marriage because they did not have children. When he got to his lodging, he made divination for them after which he advised them to make sacrifice with two snails, a cock and a hen. The women lost no time in arranging to make sacrifice. After the sacrifice, he gave them medicines to use. At the end of that month, both women became pregnant.

As soon as news of the experience of the two women circulated around, women with similar problems began to come to him and he was able to help them equally successfully. Moreover, it soon became evident that he could solve other problems apart from childlessness. He eventually became everyone's favorite and realized a lot of money and gifts which translated him to eternal fame and fortune. When he finally decided to return home, even the Oba of the town prevailed on him to stay around. He was eventually allowed to return home after promising to return.

Three years later, he returned to Ilode quietly, almost stealthily. Prior to his arrival, people had been longing for his return. As soon as the first person sighted him, he hailed on him and greeted him as their savior. There was general rejoicing when the news of his arrival went round. They began to sing his praise that people should recognize a good Awo when they saw Ugun-ogege.

If it appears as Uree at divination, the person ((if Ifa man) should be told to learn Ifa art and practice if he already has Ifa. If not, he should have his own Ifa. He should also prepare his own Osanyin because Ugun used both Ifa and medicine to perform his miracles. If the divinee is a woman, she will be advised to marry an Ifa man or persuade her husband to have his own Ifa.

The Divination He Made Before Leaving Heaven:

Akira ijo mu ro gbam gbam, was the Awo who made divination for Orunmila when he was coming to the world. He was advised to make sacrifice on account of the difficulties he was bound to encounter on earth. He was told to serve; his guardian angel with a ram for a feast, and Esu with a he-goat, a bag of money and a basket of kola nuts. He made the sacrifice but before leaving heaven, he told his guardian angel that if he succeeded as an Ifa priest on earth, he would return quickly to heaven. If he could not make it, he promised to remain for long on earth.

He subsequently left for the world and came out in the town of Ularin. On getting to Ularin, he took to trading and merely practiced Ifism on the sideline. He soon left Ularin for another town where he resumed his trading business. After his departure from Ularin, there was an out break of an epidemic of throat tumor (oligbegbe) in the town. Divine priests and physicians of all stripes and strands had been invited in vain from far and near to help in alleviating the problem. When they remembered that Irosun-Owanrin used to practice tangentially as an Ifa priest, he was invited by the people of Ularin to try his hands on the problem. When he sounded Ifa, he was told to return to Ularin to help the people.

On getting to Ularin, he made divination after which he recommended sacrifice to; Ifa with a goat and hen, and Esu with a he-goat. He went to the forest to collect Ifa leaves, adding the blood of the goat and the Iyerosun of his Ifa. After preparing the medicine, he asked everybody in the town to drink of it. Before the next morning the disease disappeared from all and sundry.

Before leaving for home, he asked for the final libation drinks and kola, but the people replied that they were not necessary because they were already well.

On getting to his new home, Esu asked him for obitayin, ogoro tayin (the post-sacrifice libation kola and drink) he replied that the people of Ularin refused to produce any. Almost immediately, Esu proclaimed that the sacrifice he made at Ularin was not accepted. Before the following morning, the incidence of throat tumor returned to the town. When they invited their diviners for divination they were told that their sacrifices were rejected because they were not complete. Their diviners declared that their only saving grace was to persuade the Ifa priest to return to the town to finalize the sacrifices. When the errand-men sent to invite him, got to his house, Irosun-Ogege bluntly refused to return because they regarded it as smacking of greed when he asked for the traditional wine and kola nuts for the finale. After persistently begging him to relent, he told them that they would have to pay one bag of money for every step he made from his house to Ularin. They agreed to his condition, which gave him a lot of money in the process.

Upon his return to the town, he asked for the same materials with which he made the sacrifice previously. He also prepared the medicine and made everybody to drink out of it. Once more, the sickness abated generally before the next morning. When he asked for the end-of-ceremony wine and kola nuts, they were quickly produced and he performed the final ritual before leaving for home. On getting home, Esu confirmed that his sacrifices were accepted.

His resounding success at Ularin spurred him to firm up a decision to revert full-time to Ifa practice, since no other business seemed capable of fetching the kind of windfall he got from the practice of Ifism. At the same time, the Divinity of Obstacle (Elenini in Yorùbá and Idoboo in Bini) went to his guardian angel to lodge a protest against the effectiveness of Irosun-Owanrin as an Ifa priest on earth.

His guardian angel reassured Elenini that since his ward promised to return early to heaven if he made it as an Ifa priest, he was due to return to heaven shortly.

Meanwhile, he became very famous and prosperous on earth as an Ifa priest. At the same time Elenini embarked on a strategy for hastening his return to heaven. The Obstacle divinity induced communal strife in a town close to his own, where people were fighting and killing one another, knowing that the people would invite Irosun-Owanrin for help.

True to expectation, the Oba of the town invited him where he made divination for them and told them to make sacrifice with 201 gourds of palm oil, 201 gourds of palm wine, 201 snails, soap worth 201 bags of money, 201 bags of salt, 201 bags of camwood, 201 pieces of white cloth and 201 packets of eko. He made the sacrifice and prepared medicine to be sprinkled round the town. Before the following morning, peace had returned to the town

When the people subsequently prepared food for him to eat, Elenini poisoned it. As soon as he ate the food, he developed throat tumor. The affliction stopped him from completing the work he went to do in the town, because he had to be rushed home. On getting home, he invited his Awos who told him that it was time for him to return to heaven, since that was his predestination. He was told however that if he wanted to prolong his stay on earth, he should make sacrifice with a ram, gourd of palm oil, and a parcel of salt. He provided the materials for the sacrifice. As he was praying with the ram in hand, it jumped up and pierced its horn into his throat tumor and as all the pus gushed out he became unconscious. While in comatose, he instantly found himself before his guardian angel in heaven.

When his guardian angel told him to fetch another ram for Elenini he replied that he had a ram tied up for sacrifice on earth. At that stage, his guardian angel told him to return to earth to complete the sacrifice. That was the point at which he regained consciousness on earth, and the ram was slaughtered without any further delay.

As soon as he became well, he gave up Ifa practice and resumed trading and farming. He consequently lived to a ripe old age. When this Ifa appears at Ugbodu, the person should be advised never to practice medicine or Ifism, if he wants to live long.

Made Divination for Sàngó and Ògún When They Fought Over a Woman:

Unknown to each other, Ògún and Sàngó were befriending the same woman. When a fight ensued between them, they invited Orunmila to resolve the matter for them. He reminded them that all three of them including the woman had earlier failed to make sacrifice. Esu later intervened to advise them to split the woman into two equal halves. Ògún took his own half and covered it on the ground. Asked what he covered up, he said it was Ijaranyin, his wife. Ijaranyin Aya Ògún - or Uja.

On his part, Sàngó took his own half and it began to ooze out water, which he called Oya.

When this Odu appears at divination for a man, he will be warned not to take interest in any other man's wife or lover. When it appears for a spinster, her parents will be advised to make sacrifice to avoid the risk of her being matcheted later by her husband for reasons of infidelity. The sacrifice will be made with a he-goat and her headgear/tie.

His Experience in Farming:

He succeeded immensely in his farming business so much so that the ram and the dog approached him to teach them the secret of his farming. He gave them land to farm on but told them to forbid the two main crops he customarily planted in his farm, which were yam and kola nut. They subsequently embarked on their own farms.

One day, the ram persuaded the dog to eat the kola nut because he had eaten the yam. Unknown to them Irosun-Owanrin had day and night watchmen guarding the farm. When the guard reported the actions of his guest-farmers to him, he made the dog to run mad and the ram to lose his voice to the point of inaudibility. They both became dumb and could no longer explain what happened to them.

When this Ifa appears at Ugbodu, the person should serve Ifa with a ram and Ogun with a dog. Thereafter he should forbid ram meat.

At divination, the person should serve Ifa with a hen and Ogun with a cock, to avoid eating what he forbids. He should however beware of friends.

Chapter **8**

IROSUN-OGUNDA
IROSUN-ATAKPO
IROSUN-EGEDAMAYAN

```
 I    I
 I    I
 I   II
II   II
```

This Odu, called Atakpo momo lere, omo bu ule jo, in heaven was specialised in making divination for people who wanted to become prosperous on earth. When he saw that all his colleagues had left for earth, he decided it was time he too came to the world.

Before leaving, he sought clearance from God, who advised him to help himself as he had done so often for others, by going for divination. He replied the Almighty Father by saying that all the Awos he would have approached had left He besought the Almighty Father to bless him and He gave him blessing, but warned that he should complement his blessing with divination and sacrifice in order to insure success for himself on earth, on account of the overbearing influence of Esu on earth.

Just before leaving for earth, he went to his guardian angel who warned him against the consequences of leaving for earth without making any sacrifice. His guardian angel however advised him to travel with a bag full of food to give to those who would accost him during his journey to earth. Even that simple advice he refused to heed, and subsequently left for the world empty-handed and without making any sacrifice.

On his way to the world, he met Emu, who asked him for food. He brushed Emu aside that he had no food to give. Emu therefore refused to follow him to the world, and he replied that he was not interested in his company. Next, he met Esu who asked him who he thought he was for daring to leave for the world without feasting anybody in heaven. He promised to give food to Esu on getting to the world.

The next divinity he met was Elenini (Idoboo) the Obstacle, who asked him for food. Once again he replied that he had no food to give. Finally, he met the Lunatic, who also asked him for food, but he replied that he had no food to offer.

He eventually entered the world, where he began by muddling up his entire life. He was very crude in his behavior and people did not take him seriously. Whenever God wanted to send him a gift, the Obstacle divinity would divert it elsewhere. Esu also made him to bemuse his life by advising him to be wearing white robes and praying every morning and evening, with the false assurance that all would be well with him. That was Esu's ploy for making it impossible for him to embark on his Ifa practice which would have enabled him to have an insight into his problems. The other Awos admonished him for deriding Ifism and of not having regard for the divinities.

Meanwhile, the Obstacle divinity sent a wife to him, who gave birth to a sickly child that made him spend all the small money he had. At a point the child died after he had spent his last money on him. That was when he decided to wander into the forest to commit suicide. At the same time, Esu decided to make him have a bird's eye view of the prosperous life he would have enjoyed if he had paid for it in heaven.

Before he could commit suicide, Esu made him to swoon into the delirious ecstasy. In the apparition, he saw his dead child, in a street strewed with every item of wealth and prosperity. He found himself in the midst of people who were rejoicing with him. In that state of euphoria, he resolved to settle in the fantasia in which he found himself in the forest. He spent seven days in that utopia in the forest, after which Esu returned him to the hard reality of the world in which he actually was, after setting his seventh heaven on fire and the resulting inferno consumed everything except his bare self. Esu woke him up only to realize that he was in the heart of the forest.

He then began to run to nowhere, but Esu once more accosted him demanding a he-goat from him. His guardian angel, who had meanwhile reproached him for failing to heed advice before leaving heaven, gave him a he-goat for Esu.

He gave the he-goat to Esu, who asked him whether he was then prepared to have regard for people stronger than himself and he replied that he was. After eating his he-goat, Esu told him to turn to one direction to meet Orunmila. He suddenly found himself back in his house.

On getting home, his Elenini-sent wife demanded a goat and pounded yam from him. He got a goat, slaughtered it and invited people for a feast. The following day, he invited Awos to come and prepare Ifa for him. When they sounded Ifa for him, they told him of the experience he had in the forest. The Ifa was prepared over a seven day period, during which he married a second wife who had several children for him. His Idoboo-sent wife left him and he became modestly prosperous and lived to a ripe old age.

When this Ifa appears at Ugbodu, the person is likely to have wandered into Christianity before having his own Ifa. He should serve Elénìnì with a goat so that his first wife would leave him, without which, he would not prosper exceedingly, because she is the agent of the Obstacle divinity.

He Made Divination for Aiye (The World):

Awerekpe una ni ijogbo, ogbologbo Oloja ni fo dem dem.
Adafafun Orunmila nijo t'on lo she awo fun aiye ni si tori omo.

It is the smoldering fire that burns the bush. It is the powerful king that speaks with force and authority. These were the Awos who made divination for Orunmila when he was going to perform Ifa for the woman called Aiye (the world) in order to have children. Orunmila was advised to make sacrifice with a he-goat. He made the sacrifice before going to divine for Aiye

At divination, he advised her to make sacrifice with an ewe (female sheep), a goat and a duck. After performing the sacrifice, he began to give her medicine, as a result of which she eventually became pregnant. In all, she had three children called: (1) Akikani-gbago (2) Ole ko mu da wa ra sh'aka and (3) Oromu romu Oshokpo.

She also had several slaves, but the most senior one was called Eyin-uwa. As soon as her children grew up as adults, Eyin-uwa left her to settle down near the sea. Long after he left her, Aiye died, and her belongings were shared among her three children. They had forgotten about Orunmila, their mother's benefactor, and Eyin-uwa, their mother's senior slave since his whereabout was unknown.

Long after the death of Aiye, Orunmila went to her children to ask them why they could not share any of their mother's belongings to him, since he was her diviner and benefactor. They however gave him a tall reply by saying that far from forgetting him, they had in fact earmarked their mother's senior slave Eyin-uwa for him, even though they had no clue on how to reach him.

Unknown to them, Eyin-uwa had done very well for himself by the side of the sea, and he became very wealthy. On getting home, Orunmila sounded Ifa to tell him how to find Eyin-uwa. He was told to give a he-goat to Esu after which he was to serve his head with a gourd of palm wine by the wayside.

He made the sacrifice to Esu. Subsequently, he took a gourd of palm wine and went to the main road leading to the town and sat down to serve his head. As he was praying to his head with kola nut and the palm wine for the return of Eyin-uwa, he saw a cavalcade of horse-riders and luggage carriers. Meanwhile, some attendants in the cortege overheard Orunmila's prayers which mentioned the name of their master at the rear of the cavalcade. They soon drew the attention of their master to what the man sitting on the roadside was saying.

Since Eyin-uwa and Orunmila knew each other previously, it was the former who recognized the latter. When he overheard Orunmila's prayers, he came down from his horse and genu-flected to pay homage to his new master, by saying that he was returning home with his retinue to pay allegiance to whoever was going to be his new master, following the death of her Mistress Aiye. Orunmila was totally flabbergasted and bewildered at the strange turn of events. They put Orunmila on one of their horses and rode home with him at the head of the procession.

Eyin-uwa who was already a prosperous man in his own right, surrendered all his wealth and fortune to Orunmila, who was translated into instant affluence.

The children of Aiye were later surprised to know how Orunmila found Eyin-uwa. When this Ifa appears at divination, the person should be advised to take good care of Orunmila. If he does not already have Ifa, he should arrange to have one. If it appears for a woman who is not yet married, she will be told that she is the wife of Orunmila.

He Made Divination for Olujati, The Father of Fishes:

Aga omode aye. Kinrindin omo sho orun. Bebele ihin, Bebele
ohun. Adafa fun Olujati ti'nshe baba eja.

Aga was the son of the world. Kinrindin was the wise man of heaven. The near side and the far side were the name of the Awos who made divination for Olujati, the father of all fishes. They advised him to make sacrifice so that human beings might not be killing his children. He was to make sacrifice with 3 cocks, 3 rats, 3 eko and 3 akara, but he refused to make it. That was why Esu alerted human beings to the nutrient value of fishes.

When it appears at divination, the person should be advised to make sacrifice to avoid losing his children to the evil machinations of the world. It is his destiny to be giving birth to children and losing them. He can only stop the incidence by having his own Ifa and if a woman, by marrying a man having his own Ifa. If the woman is already married to a non-Ifa man, she should advise him to have his own Ifa, in order to be keeping their children after giving birth to them.

Divined for Orunmila To Win The Hands of God's Daughter:

God had a beautiful daughter who was called Olose "the beauty that the eyes beholds without blinking" who was ripe for marriage. The divinities of Death and Night, each applied to marry her and God agreed to grant their request. Orunmila also applied to marry her and God also agreed. Eventually god called on them to resolve the question of which of the suitors was qualified to marry the girl.

Meanwhile, the Obstacle divinity, having obtained God's *carte blanc* to use any criterion he chose, invited the three contestants and told them that the world was already so overwhelmed with evil that anything that could be done to depopulate it was appropriate. The Obstacle divinity (Elenini) proclaimed that the first suitor to deliver a bride-prize of 201 fresh human skulls from the earth would marry the girl.

The bride-prize posed no problem for Death and the Night except for Orunmila who was not given to killing human beings. On getting home, he however sounded Ifa on what to do and he was told to make sacrifice with he-goat to Esu and to serve Ifa with a guinea-fowl and 16 snails. After serving Ifa, he was to tie the 16 shells of the snails to a forkstick and walk to the boundary of heaven and earth as soon as the first cock crowed the following morning while hitting the ground with it, he was to accompany the sound with a song to the effect that if he met death, he would fight him to a finish.

He accordingly made the sacrifice and before dawn the following morning, he took the forkstick laden with the snail's shells and left his house for the boundary of heaven and earth.

Meanwhile, Death had been to earth to procure the heads of 201 beheaded human beings, and was on his way back to heaven with the luggage. As Death approached the boundary of heaven and earth, he heard a thunderous and reverberating sound. He began to wonder what sound was so deafening. Since Death is traditionally not afraid of anyone and anything, he proceeded on his journey with characteristic bravado. As he moved nearer, he heard clearly and loudly, the defiant message borne by the song accompanying the pulsating sound which was quaking the very foundation of the earth.

Bi ma ruku ma ba ja, Iwori wo ji, Iwori wo ji wo wo !!
Bi ma ruku ma gbede, Iwori wo ji, Iwori wo ji wo wo !!! etc etc.

At that point Death stood still to assess the situation. He began to conjecture what audacious force it was that was so brazenly shaking the foundations of the earth and threatening to fight him on sight. While Death was still standing, the sound was moving nearer and nearer to him.

For the first time ever, the very divinity of Death became thoroughly scared, so much so, that he jettisoned the luggage of human skulls on his head and ran back in fright towards the earth. When Orunmila got to where Death dislodged the 201 human skulls, he dropped his snails' shell-laden forkstick and collected them for instant presentation to Elenini as his own bride-prize.

As soon as Orunmila presented the prize to Elenini, Olose was formally given in marriage to him, being the first to make his presentation. Death raced back to fetch 201 fresh human skulls from the earth because he was so sure of beating the others to it in spite of his momentary setback. He was satisfied that Orunmila had no way of procuring fresh human skulls because he was too simplistic to kill anyone. On the other hand, the Divinity of the Night would have to wait for nights unend to dream up an excuse for killing human beings before daring them.

To his utmost amazement, by the time he got to Elenini, he was told that Orunmila had already beaten him to it. Between the two losers, they swore to destroy Orunmila, for beating them handsdown. Meanwhile, Orunmila in anticipation of the inevitable backlash from his van-quished opponents decided to sound Ifa for directions. He was advised to make sacrifice with the fried meat of a rabbit and to deposit it at the last road junction before his house. He was also to roast, plantain with its skin and corn, and to deposit them at the road side. He was also to roast a whole he-goat and put the meat on the same spot.

Thereafter, Esu felt the aroma of the fried he-goat and quickly moved in to feast on it. When he saw the two other sacrifices he decided to keep watch on what was going to happen to them. The Night Divinity was the first to move in to attack Orunmila. On the approach to Orunmila's house he saw a meal of fried rabbit and could not resist the urge to feed on it. As soon as he finished eating it, Esu came out to accuse him of stealing. When the Night asked who he was supposed to have stolen from, Esu replied that the meat belonged to Orunmila. Since the penalty for theft is execution, the Night agreed to abandon his grouse against Orunmila in lieu of his meat he had eaten.

In the small hours of the morning, Death was heading for Orunmila's house with a club in hand. As soon as Esu saw him, he illuminated the roasted plantain and corn so that Death could see them clearly, being his two most forbidden taboos. As soon as Death saw the roasted corn and plantain, he abandoned his morbid intentions towards Orunmila and ran back home for safety. Orunmila was eventually left to enjoy his bride in peace and quietude.

When this Ifa appears at Ugbodu, the person will be reassured that provided he takes his Ifa fairly early, he is going to do very well in life. He is likely to be involved in a love contest for a woman with two other men. He should make similar sacrifices as those referred to above. He should forbid plantain roasted with its skin.

The Incantation For Marriage:

Orunmila ni atapo ni momo lere.

Moni olomo ba ile jo.
Moron tolu, Mokun won ton lerin.
Akuko adiye ki ge igi, be ni ki i gba emu
tio fi ri iyawo.
Ogbo eyele ki ni kan sun, Oun taya ni yio ma sun.
Oun taya ni yio maa ji.

Meaning:

The dividend from a marriage investment is childbirth.
It is a productive wife that fills the house with children.
I will have you as a wife to bear children for me.
Because the cock neither chops fire wood, nor presents, before having a wife.
An elderly pigeon does not sleep alone.
He sleeps and wakes with his wife.

Children born out of this marriage shall be called:- Amosun, Ifatumise, Ifasanmi, Ifayemisi, Ifajemite, Ifaponle, Ifayemi, Ifagbemiga, Ifakolade.

When this odù appears at divination for a man, he will be advised that Ifa will fetch the right woman for him to marry. If it appears for a woman, she will be told that the man who is currently proposing to her is her correct husband.

He Made Divination for The Pineapple:

Je ki mi fi'di he. Let me sit properly, was the name of the Awo who made divination for the Pineapple (Ekinkun) when she was looking for a suitable abode conducive to productivity. She was told to make sacrifice with 200 needles, cotton wool, rabbit and kola nuts.

After making the sacrifice, the Ifa priest gave her two kola nuts to hold with her wherever she went. She was told that wherever she felt like sitting down, she should say to people "may I please be allowed to sit down and serve my head here"? She was told that whoever gave her permission to sit down, would be her husband, who would give her peace of mind and a chance to bear children.

She visited several places without obtaining permission to settle down. Meanwhile, the hilltop was told at divination to make sacrifice with 2 cocks on account of a woman who was coming to make a request on him. After the sacrifice he was advised to agree to any request the woman would make on him.

When the pineapple eventually got to the hilltop (apata in Yorùbá) she sought and obtained permission to sit down to serve her head. As she was serving her head, Esu used the cotton wool with which she made sacrifice to glue her buttocks to the hilltop. As she tried to stand up after serving her head, she discovered that her buttocks had been glued to the ground. The hill subsequently asked her why she was in a hurry to leave, while persuading her to resume her seat to keep him company.

At bed time, Apata drew nearer to her and made love to her. She however told Apata that she had just finished her menstruation the previous day. She subsequently became pregnant. That is why pineapples grow on hilltops.

When it appears at divination for a man, he will be advised to make sacrifice so that his predestined wife will come to him. If he makes sacrifice, he will recognize and readily accept her lest, he will miss her, and the path of his destiny. When making the sacrifice, the Ifa priest will add the leaves of pineapple to the materials.

Chapter **9**

IROSUN-OSA

```
II   I
I    I
I    II
I    II
```

He Made Divination for The Cock Before Marrying The Hen:

Eke kukuru, ika gbooro.
Adifa fun akiko mo galaja nijo
t'onlo she oko abo.

He made divination for the cock when he was going to take the hen for a wife. He told the cock to make sacrifice with rat, fish, akara, eko and kola nuts. He made the sacrifice and the hen offered no resistance to his proposal for marriage.

When the Ifa appears at divination, the person should be told to make sacrifice to avoid the risk of losing his life on account of a woman. If it appears for a woman, she will be told to make sacrifice, so that two men may not fight because of her, and for the safety of her children.

He Made Divination for The Knife:

Irosun Sasasa awo abe, odifa fun abe.

He made divination for the knife when he was going to shave the head of Orisa. He was told to make sacrifice to avoid doing the work in half measure. He did not do the sacrifice. Without doing the sacrifice, he left the next day to shave the hair of Orisa.

On his way, Esu confronted him with a chance to earn additional money by first cutting his own hair. He told Esu that his first priority was to shave Orisa's hair. Eventually, Esu succeeded in persuading him to shave his hair. But as he was shaving Esu's hair, it was growing instantaneously. The cutting lasted the whole day and yet, he had made no significant impact. At dusk, Esu's hair was as bushy as it was before the cutting started. Consequently, Esu refused to pay because his hair was not shaved. The knife raised no qualms because he drew a casual connection between the sacrifice he failed to make and his abortive experience. When he got home that evening, he proceeded to make the sacrifice.

Thereafter, he was able to get to Orisa's house the following morning to cut his hair. When Orisa queried him for failing to turn up the previous day, he explained by narrating his unavailing experience on his way to honor the appointment.

When it appears at divination, the person should be advised to make sacrifice to avoid obstacle in his job. For a woman, she will be advised to make sacrifice to avoid problems in her marriage from her husband or children.

He Made Divination for Fire:

Irosun sa ara ga. He made divination for Fire, advising him to make sacrifice to avoid losing his wife, Po. He was told to make sacrifice with a red cock, red cloth and palm oil. He refused to make the sacrifice because he could neither imagine his wife leaving him nor anyone daring to seduce her from him.

His wife Po, was also advised to make sacrifice with her wearing apparel to avoid getting into trouble. She too refused to make the sacrifice. Subsequently, she ran away from the husband's house to live with the grass of the bush. Fire did not make any move because the event happened during the rainy season. He waited for the dry season to emerge. At the appearance of the dry season, Fire put on his red clothes and stood at the edge of the bush calling on the grass to return his wife or face his wrath. The grass replied that he should do his worst. Fire reacted by burning up all the plants and animals in the bush.

When this odù appears at divination, the man should be warned not to seduce anybody's wife because it could cost him his life.

He Made Divination for The Hawk (Asa or Ahua):

He made divination for the Hawk when Orisa withdrew his hunting weapon after he had cheated. Orisa had given a pair of scissors to the Hawk to be hunting for him. The Hawk however developed the habit of flying about all day only to report mission unaccomplished to Orisa. Thereafter, the Hawk would proceed for his own hunting, in which he was invariably successful. When Orisa realized that the Hawk was cheating, he invited him to bring his hunting weapon for refurbishment. Far from re-sharpening the scissors, Orisa actually seized it.

Thereafter, the Hawk began to starve from lack of hunting weapons. Being too ashamed to return to Orisa, he decided to go for divination. He was told to make sacrifice with a cock and a he-goat. Orunmila gave the cock to Ogun to prepare a new pair of scissors for the Hawk. Ogun produced the scissors and gave it to Orunmila, who prepared the iyerosun to magnetize it, such that anything or game it held would be glued to it.

With his new weapon, the Hawk was able to resume successful hunting. When it appears at Ugbodu, the head of a hawk and the appropriate leaves are used to prepare a blacksmith's scissors on the skull of a gorilla for the person to keep on his Ifa shrine, to enable him to achieve his objective in life.

The Divination He Made Before Leaving Heaven:

Mikoligho kirin, mo ko ligho kirin. Omo eku okirin ka abare
odukuluku odi baba eka. Ono eja kirin ka aba re. Odi baba re
ja. Mi ko ligho kirin, mi ghrigho kirin. Oduro kpekpe. Okirin
ka aba re. Odu kulukulu, odi baba re kin.

When he asked for the sacrifice to make before leaving heaven, he was told to; feast his guardian angel with a castrated he-goat, serve Esu with he-goat, and Ogun with cock, tortoise and dog. He was told that the sacrifice was necessary for ameliorating the problems awaiting him on earth. He was also told to serve unknown enemies in the forest with dog, cock and his torn clothes. He made all the sacrifices and he sought and obtained the blessing of God before leaving for earth with chalk, white cloth and eagle's feather. He had also been told to make sacrifice to the Obstacle divinity, but he was too tired to remember to do it.

He got to the world to see that there was already enlightenment. He did not demonstrate that he was an Awo although people suspected he was one. He began by serving his fellow Awos without ignoring anyone of them. He later found himself in the household of the Oba of the town. While in the palace, he was quietly practicing Ifa for other people. Meanwhile, the Obstacle divinity he failed to serve in heaven, began to disrupt his activities by damaging the things put under his charge in the palace, which were the medicinal and diabolical protective devices of the Oba. When the Oba discovered the damage done to his most cherished belongings, he demanded an explanation from Irosun-Osa. The Oba did not execute him being an Awo, but confiscated all his belongings, expelled him from the palace, and banished him into exile.

He spent his first few months of exile in the forest because he had no clothes to wear in a human habitat. He began to live with animals, to which he demonstrated his benevolence. When Esu saw how he was suffering, he went to Ogun and his guardian angel in heaven to query them for allowing him to suffer so much deprivation on earth, in spite of the sacrifices he made before leaving heaven. His guardian angel explained that he was destined to be an Ifa priest, but that he abandoned the practice of Ifism and began to serve other people, when he ought to be leading.

Esu subsequently met him to demand a he-goat, which he brought out from his Akpominijekun. After eating the he-goat, Esu directed him to an Ifa priest who was visiting the earth from heaven. That was at the boundary of heaven and earth. The Awo made divination for Irosun-Osa and reminded him that he vowed in heaven to be a practicing Ifa priest on earth. The Awo directed him to return to the bush to collect whatever he saw at the place where he had been sleeping. On getting there, he saw a sledge hammer which Ogun had mean while kept there for him.

The Awo from heaven had told him to serve whatever he found with a cock and also to serve his own Ifa with a ram. When he returned to his forest abode, he could not find his Ifa seeds (Ikin). He however saw some Ikin spread out as if they had just been prepared but did not touch them. He neither picked up Ogun's sledge hammer gift nor the Ifa he saw lined out. While he was sleeping that night, his guardian angel told him that he should collect the Ifa seeds he saw because they were his own and also Ogun's gift of a sledge hammer and to make sacrifices to them to mark the beginning of his Ifa practice.

He made the sacrifices and began to practice Ifa art for whoever took him seriously enough to come to him. Incidentally, all his predictions came true and all his sacrifices manifested, which began to direct more and more clients to him. The Awos from heaven had also advised him to serve the Obstacle divinity with all eatable materials and a dog. He finally made the sacrifice after which Elénìnì removed the roadblock with which he had held up his prosperity in heaven.

There was a remarkable swing in fortune for him after that final sacrifice. The daughter of Olókun came from heaven to meet him for divination. After divining for her, the woman refused to leave him, offering instead to marry him. Subsequently, the woman brought her slaves and assets from the palace of her father, which made them become vastly wealthy. He was soon afterwards, able to build a house of his own.

At the same time Esu went to the town where he had lived with the Oba and caused lots of problems for them. The difficulties lasted for three years during which their solution defied the skill and expertise of all the invited Awos. Eventually, the Awo from heaven met the Oba of the town and told him that the problem arose on account of the Awo he banished ignominiously from his domain.

He was told that it was only that Awo who could solve the problems of the town.   Almost immediately, the Oba made a proclamation that Irosun-Osa should be searched for and persuaded to return to the town. Professional searchers (uwamuwa in Yorùbá and omu-ama in Bini) were sent to locate his whereabouts. The professional searchers succeeded in targeting him and subsequently made a rendezvous with him.

When they however told him that the Oba wanted to see him, he bluntly refused to accept the invitation. He insisted that he was expelled and forced to go into exile in disdainful circumstances because the Oba had no more use for him. He eventually told them that before he could return to the town, the Oba should send him a castrated he-goat, dog, cock, white cloth, rat and fish for sacrifice.

When the message was given to the Oba he quickly ordered the materials to be sent to him. After getting them, he served; Esu with the he-goat, his Ifa with the castrated he-goat, rat and fish, and Ogun with the cock and dog. Thereafter he left to go and see the Oba. On getting to the palace, he made divination for the Oba and told him that the secondary divinity of the town called Osa had not been served for almost seven years since the death of its last priest. The shrine was immediately refurbished and the divinity was served with a goat, a ram, a cock and plenty of food and drinks. Almost immediately afterwards, the problems which had been besetting the town began to abate following a rainstorm. There had been a drought in the town for three years. Eventually, when the sacrifice was being made, someone got possessed and professed that peace and prosperity would return finally to the town if Irosun-Osa could be successfully persuaded to become the next chief priest of the reanimated Osa divinity. After ordering a befitting house to be built for him, the Oba succeeded in convincing Irosun-Osa to return to the town. His return to the town marked the beginning of the reappearance of peace and prosperity for all and sundry. He lived to a ripe old age in relative opulence. He became famous for making prophecies that unfailingly came true.

When this Ifa appears at Ugbodu, the person should be told that he had ignored Ifa for too long.

He should immediately prepare Esu and Ogun for his Ifa and serve the reanimated Ifa with a castrated he-goat. He will prosper in the land of his birth.

His Final Divination for The Oba:

About seven years after his return to the town of Igbajo, he had a curious dream in which the Oba was removed from the throne. While he was contemplating whether or not to alert the Oba with his misgivings, he decided to make divination at which he was told to serve his head with chalk and salt beseeching his head to lead him to his final destination in life. He did the sacrifice and left for the palace.

On getting there, he made divination for the Oba, advising him to serve his head with the meat of an elephant to obviate the danger of being removed from the throne. The Oba became so annoyed that he ordered the immediate arrest and detention of Irosun-Osa for daring to predict the remote possibilty of his dethronement. The Oba had forgotten how all the previous predictions of Irosun-Osa used to come true with textbook exactitude. Instead of making the prescribed sacrifice, the Oba felt relieved after incarcerating the diviner into detention.

Five days later, the town of Igbajo was attacked by enemy forces and the Oba was removed and subsequently sent to an unknown destination. He was later reported to have been killed.

Finding themselves without an Oba, the kingmakers were invited by the people to make divination on the appointment of a new Oba. All the seven diviners invited unanimously recommended that the Awo who was in detention should be released and crowned as the new Oba, because he alone could return peace and tranquility back to Igbajo.

When this Ifa appears at Ugbodu, the person should immediately serve his head with white chalk mixed with salt, coconut, white kola nut and a white cock. He should give he-goat immediately to Esu and persevere in whatever suffering he encounters because God will compensate him with a great favor in the end. At divination, the person should also serve his head with a cock in order to obtain an expected favor.

Chapter **10**

IROSUN-ETURA
IROSUN-AJALA

```
I    I
II   I
I   II
I   II
```

Orunmila Names The Most Successful Tree in The Forest:

Orunmila ni o kara, Emi na ni o koro.
Orunmila ni oni gbajumo a de. Moni tani oni gbajumo.
Moni iroko kon om be lo oko o yi, moni oun lo gbajumo.
Orunmila ni iro ni, ki'nshe lo gbajumo.

O runmila asked the Ifa priest to name the most prosperous tree in the forest. The Ifa priest mentioned the Iroko tree and the oak tree. Orunmila said they were not. When he put the question once more, the Ifa priest replied that he had no clue. Orunmila subsequently declared the palm tree as the most prosperous tree in the forest, because, it leaves are money (brooms) its wine is money (palm wine) its fruit are money (palm oil) the chaff of its fruits after producing oil is money (chaff igniting fire), its seeds are money, (palm kernel oil) the chaff from its seeds is money (for animal feeds), and the shells from its seeds are money for (reinforcing construction work). Orunmila said that there was no other tree in the forest whose entire body was money-producing.

When this Odu appears at divination, the person should be told to have his own Ifa in order to prosper in life. If he is not in a position to have his own Ifa, he should serve; Ifa with a hen and a pigeon, and Esu with a he-goat, in order to prosper and become famous in life.

The Divination He Made Before Leaving Heaven:

Ajala aiye, ajala orun, were the two Awos who made divination for this odù before he left heaven for earth. He was advised to make sacrifice because he was going to be a practicing Ifa priest on earth, and on account of the difficulties he was going to encounter in the hands of the elderly Awos. He was told to give; a ram, 24 pigeons, a tortoise, the meat of bush goat (edu in Yorùbá and oguonziran in Bini) and seed yam to his guardian angel, he-goat to Esu, and to obtain God's blessing with a piece of white cloth, 21 pieces of white chalk, red parrot's feather and a basket of 201 coconuts. He made all the sacrifices before leaving for the world.

He met a number of elderly awos on earth, but was engaged in his own practice quietly. Meanwhile, the Oba of his town. Owo, where he came out, became ill. The Awo who traditionally took care of the Olowo of Owo was called Ajana-oko, a very old man. When the Oba's illness defied the efforts of Ajana-oko, he ordered that all accessible Awos should be invited to help him. Ajana-oko had been told to serve Esu with he-goat and the meat of bush goat, but he failed to do it. He subsequently went to the forest one day and saw that his trap had caught a bush goat. He took it home to put the meat on the drier. At the same time, Irosun-Etura was told at a morning divination to serve; Esu with a he-goat and his head with 201 pieces of coconut and a pigeon, and his Ifa with the meat of bush goat. He did all the sacrifices, but could not obtain bush goat with which to serve his Ifa. He therefore improvised with wine and kola nuts, promising to use bush goat as soon as he could get it.

After eating his he-goat from Irosun-Etura, later to be nicknamed Ajana-Ule, Esu went to stoke the anus of Ajana-oko for failing to make sacrifice and immediately, while on his way to the palace, he developed diarrhea, which soon turned to cholera. By the time he arrived at the palace, he was almost dying. The Oba was told of Ajana-oko's condition and he was figuring out what to do when Esu in the guise of a visiting elder statesman, advised him to send for a young hitherto unknown awo called Irosun-Etura for help. The Oba immediately sent for him. When he sounded Ifa on the invitation, he was cleared to go, because he was going to return from there with honor and dignity.

On getting to the palace, he was immediately asked to do what he could to save the life of Ajana-oko. When he split the welcome kola nut presented to him and threw it for divination, he declared that Ajana-oko had failed to make the sacrifice prescribed for him to serve Esu with a he-goat and his Ifa with the meat of a bush goat. He declared that the man did not make the sacrifice even though he was drying up a whole bush goat in his house. Ajana-oko was perplex at the precision with which the young awo pinpointed his problems.

Ajana-oko confirmed that he was actually drying up in his house, the bush goat caught by his trap. The Oba immediately gave orders for the bush goat to be fetched from Ajana-oko's house for the sacrifice while also providing a he-goat for Esu. As soon as the sacrifice was made, Ajana-oko became well.

Following his remarkable success he achieved in healing Ajana-oko, the Oba invited Irosun-Etura to look into his own long-standing illness as well. After divination and sacrifice, the young awo at last succeeded in making the Oba well. The Oba was surprised to know that such a highly competent and talented Ifa priest lived in his domain without his knowledge. The Oba gave him the nickname of Ajana-ule and confirmed him at once as the chief Royal Diviner of Owo. He became very popular. At the height of his success, a wife was betrothed to him, who incidentally was a witch, who was to cooperate with his detractors to ferment problems for him.

His problems began when his wife through witchcraft seized his masculine potency and he could no longer make love. Up to that time he had no child. As he was however sleeping one night he had a dream in which his guardian angel queried him for neglecting his Ifa practice after taking a chieftaincy title and marriage. His guardian angel told him to find out what sacrifice to make to subdue his wife because the woman was too strong for him.

When he woke up in the morning, he sounded Ifa on the significance of his dream and he was told to serve Esu with a he-goat, adding the flames coming out of bonfire (majala in Yorùbá and ebibi-eren in Bini), roasted corn and seed yam. He made the sacrifice and the Ifa preparation was tied at the entrance to his house. After the sacrifice, Esu went to the meeting of witches and caused a rift among them. They all fought till day break and a spate of open confession ensued. His wife confessed that she was responsible for arresting her husband's potency. She disclosed that she was being forced meanwhile, to return the husband's potency to him.

The matter was subsequently remitted to the Oba who ordered that the wife of Ajana-ule should be executed by offering her as sacrifice to the ground divinity. His subsequent marriages were happy and productive. The wife had confessed the names of the elderly Awos who suborned her to attack her husband because he had stolen the show from them. All the Awos mentioned in the confession were made to go on trial by ordeal and they were all caught and subsequently died one after the other.

When this Ifa appears at Ugbodu, the person should be told never to marry a woman procured for him except one chosen by himself. The problem of impotence is one for which the special sacrifice has to be made for him without delay. He will be very successful in his job, but success will generate envy and enmity for him. He should make sacrifice.

Divination Made for Ogun:

> Ofaso bo ri oso, Ogbe bu ika ton agbalagba to kpe ibu ika.
> Ori arare ni yio hule. Adafa fun Ogun nijo tio teja fun Ogun.

The person who covered his face with a cloth when he fouled the air. The man who sews evil will reap evil - were the Awos who made divination for Orunmila when he was going to prepare Ifa for Ogun at the insistence of Orisa-Nla. Orunmila refused to do it because he said "Ewe t'ashe ki'ru, Oro to a mo tele ki'ni lara" That is, "A severed leaf does not grow again.

An information already known is not difficult to narrate." That was his figure of speech for predicting that Ogun would repay his good turn with ingratitude. At the insistence of Orisa-Nla, Orunmila prepared Ifa for Ogun and through to his earlier prediction, Ogun repaid him with crass ingratitude.

When it appears at divination, the person should be advised not to repay a good turn with ingratitude, lest he would suffer immensely and he would be cursed and no on would ever be able to revoke it. Whether a man or a woman, the divinee is a ingrate.

The Divination Made for Orunmila When Òrìsà Sent Ogun To Fight Him:

A fi igba korodo gbon odo ino ngbon le ori agbalagba i to ba gbe'bu ika, yio hu ni ori omo re ni ola. These were the Ifa priests who made divination for Òrúnmìlà when Òrìsà-tolu-yeb-gbe, the husband of Yemowo requested Ogun to fight Orunmila to a finish. Orunmila's fame and popularity had come to earn him the displeasure of all other diviners around. After his fellow Ifa priest had tried and failed to fight him, it was the turn of the divine chiefs to have a go at him. Orisa-tolu-yegbe procured the high priest of the Ogun divinity to embark on a crusade for eliminating Irosun-Etura for stealing the show from everybody.

At his usual morning divination. Ifa warned Irosun-Etura that more powerful enemies were plotting to fight him. He was told to make sacrifice with white cloth, he-goat, and parrot's feather. He made the sacrifice. Meanwhile, Ogun told Orisa-tolu-yegbe that he did not know the way to Orunmila's house in Owa town. Orisa-tolu-yegbe gave Ogun the description of Orunmila's house as the one having a palm frond in front of it in the quarter called Ona-Iranya.

After enjoying the sacrifice, Esu altered the descriptions and locations. What Orisa-tolu-yegbe did not tell Ogun was that he (Orisa) also lived in the same locality. On the night that Ogun was to attack, Esu transposed the palm frond in front of Orunmila's house with the white cloth in front of Orisa-tolu-yegbe's house.

As soon as the first cock crowed in the early hours of the morning, Ogun went to Owo and began to search for the house with a palm frond in the front of it in the Ona-Iranya quarters. As soon as Ogun located the house, he started killing all the inmates he came across. When the children of Orisa-tolu-yegbe saw what of the girl than the crude Onobule. His friend was often outtalking him and gaining more attention from the girl.

As soon as Onobule began to have the cold shoulders from the girl, he went to Orunmila for divination and he was told that he was going to lose his fiance to another man unless he made sacrifice. He was told to; give he-goat to Esu, rabbit to night, and serve his head at the foot of a palm tree with a guinea-fowl. He made the sacrifices. Not knowing that his friend was the rival scheming to overthrow him, in his characteristic naivete, he went to tell his friend what he was told at divination.

When he was subsequently going to the girl's place, he again invited his friend to accompany him. On getting there, they were served with palm wine. As the friend was drinking, Esu blinked his eyes to him and he became tipsy. In his delirium, he confessed that he had been scheming to seduce the girl from Onobule. His confession angered the parents of the girl into giving the girl to Onobule right away. The Night did their own bit by making him to fall deeply asleep when all the nuptial ceremonies were taking place.

When it appears at Ugbodu and at divination, the person should be told not to be too trusting with friends. He should be advised to give he-goat to Esu and to serve his head with guinea-fowl while backing Ifa shrine so that close associates might not deprive him of his rightful entitlement.

The Divination Made for Him Before Leaving Heaven:

Efun fun Lere - was the Awo who made divination for Orunmila when he was leaving heaven. He was advised not to practice Ifa on earth but to take to trading. He was told to make sacrifice with sixteen pigeons, a goat, a piece of white cloth and 201 cowries to his guardian angel. He was also told to serve Esu with a he-goat, corn, yam, plantain and cocoyam. He made all the sacrifices before leaving for the world.

On getting to the world, he began to practice Ifism, but did not have a settled life. He was otherwise very effective as an Ifa priest, but he did not prosper by it. When he subsequently went for divination, he was told that he had strayed away from the path of his destiny, and that he was supposed to have taken to trading. He was told to serve Ifa by decorating its shrine with white chalk and white cloth. He was told to serve Olókun with a pigeon, a bag of cowries, money, and chalk, and to serve Esu with a he-goat, corn, yam, plantain and cocoyam. He did all the sacrifices.

When Olókun received the sacrifice, he remembered the sacrifice which Irosun-Ofun made to him in heaven and the pledge of support he made to him. Olókun reacted by dispatching his fair-skinned daughter, dressed in white apparel to look for Irosun-Ofun at Oja-ajigbomekon. At the same time, Irosun-Ofun was told to dress in white clothes when going to the market. When Olókun's daughter got to the market, she was the centre of attraction, but spoke to nobody. She was looking for the man dressed in white clothes as her father told her.

Not long afterwards, Irosun-Ofun, also dressed in white, met Olókun's daughter and they fell in love at once. When he introduced himself, she offered to follow him to his house. When she got to his house to see the white decoration and adornment all around, she told him that his house provided a suitable environment for her to stay. He soon discovered that the only food she ate was white chalk, which gave him an idea of who she was.

Meanwhile, the woman advised him to be dressing always in white and to be following her o the market. On every market day, her servants brought wares from heaven to sell on earth, after which she was given the money realized from the sales. On the following market day her servants came with beads, jewels and elephant tusks which were all sent to Orunmila's house. Most of the materials brought by Olókun's servants, had previously not been seen any where on earth. The Oba of the town was subsequently attracted by them and he bought some of the from Orunmila at a prize of 200 men and 200 women.

Chapter **11**

IROSUN-IRETE
IROSUN-OKPINI
IROSUN-ERO

```
 I    I
 I    I
II   II
 I   II
```

The Divination He Made Before Leaving Heaven:

Aperin nia mowodudu. Agbe toko bo ri shi o shio. Those were the two Awos who made divination for this odù before he left heaven for earth. He was advised to serve; Esu with he-goat; his guardian angel with a goat, hen, pigeon, tortoise, snail, rat fish and guinea-fowl; and the Obstacle divinity with corn, plantain, yam, cock, gourd of water and a pack of firewood at the junction of heaven and earth. He made the sacrifice before leaving for the world.

On getting to the world he was practicing Ifa art on a full time basis. He was very successful because his generosity and reasonableness brought him many clients. When the traditional Awos who were often charging exorbitant fees for their work were no longer having enough to do, his enemies in heaven went to report him to God that he was disrupting the peace of the world. The Obstacle divinity (Elenini or Idoboo) was appointed by God to verify the situation of things on earth. Thereafter, Elenini decided to visit the world to investigate what was happening. Before leaving for the world, he sent a message to all the divinities that he was coming to do battle with all those responsible for allowing evil to flourish on earth.

When Ogun got Elenini's message, he raised a huge army to make a preemptive strike against Elenini's imminent attack. On knowing about Ogun's contrivance for preemptive action, he sat on the road and pulled back the hat he was wearing. The action effectively blocked all passage, thus preventing anyone from passing through. Ogun and his army arrived to discover the roadblock and they could not pass through, because the blockade was axe-and-machete proof.

After struggling in vain to get through, they became tired. That was when Elenini turned his face to them to ask what they were trying to do. When Ogun explained that they were going to fight the forces of Elenini from heaven, he commanded Ogun and his troops to turn into a leaf which he kept in his bag.

Sàngó was the next to rise to the occasion. When he too met Elenini, he turned him into a stone which he kept in his bag. All the other ferocious divinities suffered the same fate in the hands of Elenini. Meanwhile, Orunmila sounded Ifa on how to deal with the approaching calamity, and he was told to prepare a feast with a goat in anticipation of the approaching heavenly forces. He was also advised to raise a procession of dancers, to welcome, instead of combatting them.

Subsequently, Orunmila prepared food and drinks at home and led his entire household after rubbing the chalk of peace on their faces, and they sang and danced to meet the strongest divinity created by God. They were not only singing in praise of Elenini but also calling him the strongest of all divinities and mortals. When Elenini heard the noise from the dancing and singing of Òrúnmìlà's retinue, he once more turned his cap to block the road.

Orunmila got to the road block without knowing what to do. He however continued to sing and dance until Elenini was satisfied that they did not come to fight but to make peace. He subsequently turned his face to ask who they were and Orunmila replied that he was the divinity of wisdom, and that he came to welcome him to earth. When Elenini told Orunmila to enter his bag, he invited the Obstacle divinity to his house for the feast prepared for him. He promised to enter the bag after he must have dined and wined because he must have been hungry from his long trip. Elenini was meanwhile enjoying the singing and dancing and was quite happy to ac-company Orunmila to his house.

He arrived at Orunmila's house to find a table laid for a sumptuous feast. He ate and drank to his heart's content. After eating and drinking, Elenini asked for a repeat performance of the singing and dancing. As they were all dancing, Elenini faced Orunmila, telling him that he came to the world because God had been told that he (Orunmila) was spoiling the world. He observed that he was satisfied that far from spoiling the world, he was the only one who was striving to make it habitable. He concluded that he was leaving him on earth to continue with his good works, but that he was going with all the other divinities in his bag to heaven.

After expressing his gratitude for appreciating his humble gestures, Orunmila observed that he could not enjoy life as a loner on earth. He begged for the release of the other divinities. In deference to the entreaties of Orunmila, Elenini released the others warning them from then on to refrain from evil behavior.

If this Ifa appears at Ugbodu, the person should be told to make elaborate sacrifice because he was destined to be very wealthy, provided he keeps a good heart and humane disposition. When it appears at divination for a person who has a pending case, he will be advised to serve Esu with a he-goat in order to receive a favorable judgement.

The Divination Made for Him When He Was Going To Olofin:

Okpini omosin, Okpini omo ora. Okpini okpe'ron
ja le de. Okpini ofo akpoko lo'ko. Okpini ofo
akpere le re. Okpini fo akpe ekun gbogbo jekun jeron je.
I am the one who can put good blood in people's body.
I am the one who can make things happen.
To substantiate my assertion, a boa, a python and a tiger
    will be killed today.
If it does not manifest, I will throw away my Ikin and

other instruments of divination.

Olofin's favorite wife had no child and he had invited all known Awos at home and abroad to help without success. When he heard of the famous Irosun-Irete of Oke-jetti he invited him.

When Irosun-Irete got Olofin's message, he sounded Ifa on what to do. He was told to serve Ifa with a he-goat before going on. His wife told him not to wait for the sacrifice before answering Olofin's invitation and that he could make it on his return. He accepted his wife's suggestion and left for the palace without making the sacrifice.

On getting there, he made divination, after which he confirmed that Olofin's wife would become pregnant within three months, provided he was able to make sacrifice to his Ifa with a boa, a Python and a tiger, and to serve Esu with a he-goat. As Olofin was imaging how he was going to obtain the reptiles and animal for the sacrifice, Irosun-Irete reassured him by predicting that three of his hunters would return with the three materials on that very day. He promised to throw his Ikin away if his prediction did not come true. He then left for home after telling Olofin to send for him as soon as the hunters showed up.

True to his prediction, three of Olofin's hunters actually respectively killed a boa, a python and a tiger on that day, but to punish the soothsayer for listening to his wife without making sacrifice, Esu accosted the hunters on their way home and told them that an Ifa priest had predicted to the Olofin that morning, that any hunter who reported with a boa, a python and a tiger on that day, should in addition to the games be used to make sacrifice to enable Olofin's favorite wife to become pregnant. For fear of losing their lives, the three hunters threw away their games and took refuge at the foot of a big tree.

After waiting in vain for the hunters to show up, Olofin became annoyed and sent for Irosun-Irete to tell him that his prediction did not materialize.

Almost immediately after that, the Ifa priest threw his ikin into the lake near Olofin's palace. After disgracing him and allowing him to throw his principal divination instrument away, Esu once more transfigured into a hunter and went to meet the three royal hunters at their hiding place. After exchanging pleasantries, they identified themselves and told their fellow hunter why they were hiding for fear of losing their lives. The Esu-turned-hunter told them that there was no threat whatsoever to their lives, and that on the contrary, the Olofin had been expecting them to report with their games all day. He reassured them by saying that they would come with those games on that day and that each of them should be rewarded respectively with money, a wife and a chieftaincy title.

Esu directed them to where they had earlier dumped their games, and after retrieving them, he accompanied them to the palace. Olofin was very happy to see them and they explained their late arrival by saying that someone came to the forest to deceive them with the wrong information when they were coming to the palace earlier with their games. Almost immediately, Olofin sent at once for Irosun-Irete. He however refused to honor the invitation on the ground that having thrown away his Ifa, he was no longer going to practice as an Ifa priest.

Olofin however got one of his royal mariners to dive into the lake to retrieve the Ifa seeds (ikin).

As the mariner first dive into the lake, he came up with five seeds. His second plunge brought out another five, then three, two, and finally, one. This is the origin of how the Ifa priest selects seeds for Ikin divination. After retrieving the Ifa seeds, Olofin sent another message to Irosun-Irete to confirm that his Ifa had successfully been salvaged from the lake.

Eventually, he returned to the palace to perform the sacrifice. At the end of that month, Olofin's favorite wife actually became pregnant. Olofin demonstrated his appreciation with plenty of gifts and a chieftaincy title. He then sang in praise of Orunmila.

When this Ifa appears at divination, the person should be told to serve Esu with a he-got before leaving for an important engagement.

His Affray With The Elders of The Night:

Due to the fact that he often delayed in making sacrifices, because he was in the habit of using the materials with which his clients made sacrifices, to make his own sacrifices, which of course were never accepted. He had a hen which used to lay eggs and hatch chickens regularly.

On one occasion, the hen laid nine eggs. Meanwhile, Awon Iyami Osoronga (elders of the night) also stacked their eggs near those of his fowl. The fowl subsequently kept the witches' eggs with its own. In the ensuing quarrel, the witches rejected their eggs. He later collected all the eggs, but he was soon taken ill and when he made divination, he was told to send a rabbit and three eggs to the elders of the night. After making the offering, he became well. It was from then on that those making sacrifices to the night were often required to add three eggs, to pay for the eggs rejected by Awon-Iyami Osoronga.

When this Ifa appears at Ugbodu, the person should send a hen and three eggs to the elders of the night. At divination, the person should give a he-goat to Esu.

He Made Divination for Ariku:

Atori a budi gbejegi. Odifa fun Ariku nu ojo ti o fe lo
da Ifa oun danu.

The squirrel's stick (Uwenriontan in Bini and Atori in Yorùbá) with a thick base, was the name of the Ifa priest who made divination for Ariku when he was about to throw his Ifa away. Ariku was very poor when he was told to have his own Ifa. Since he had no money, he borrowed to fund the ceremony. After having the Ifa, he was told that he would begin to prosper after three years.

Meanwhile, those who lent the money to him began to demand repayment. It was three months to the third anniversary of having his Ifa. At that stage, he was already so frustrated that he lost confidence in the veracity of the three-year gestation.

That was because he saw no signs of approaching prosperity. He then went to Atori abudi gbejegi, the Awo who prepared the Ifa for him to complain that he saw no signs of an imminent manifestation of his prediction. The man advised him to exercise a little more patience.

When it was fifteen days to the third anniversary of his Ifa, his patience had reached its terminus. He collected his Ifa and packed it up to go and throw away. In heaven, his guardian angel went to appeal to God to grant him permission to go and warn Ariku not to behave stupidly to ruin his life. God granted his request and the guardian angel instantly turned into a bird and flew to meet Ariku on his way to where he was going to throw his Ifa away. After flying round him, the bird began to beat his body with its wings, while singing:

Ariku maa da'fu nu, jenje,
Aje t'oun fe bo le yin, jenje,
Ariku maa di fa nu, jenje,
Aya t'onfe bo le yin, jenje.
Ariku ma da fa nu, jenje,
Omo t'onfe bo leyin, jenje.
Ariku maa difa nu, jenje,
Gbogbo ola re bo le yin, jenge.

The bird advised him not to throw his Ifa away because all the ingredients of prosperity were on their way to him.

With that reassurance, Ariku returned home with his Ifa. On the 15th day, people came to him for divination, and his predictions all came to pass. The daughter of Aje led the team to his house for divination. He told the woman that she was the wife of Orunmila and she confirmed that she came with her followers to live with him as a wife. Within a period of three months he became very wealthy. Before the next anniversary of his Ifa, he had built a house and had a child from his wife. His days of penury were over.

When this odù appears at divination, the person should be told to make sacrifice with a he-goat, cock and hen, and told to exercise patience because his prosperity is in the offing.

He Made Divination for Okpini When He Was Going To Olofin:

Tikpini, Tikpini awo Okpini. Odifa fun Okpini ni ojo to
fe lo she awo fun Olofin.

He made divination for Okpini when he was going to make divination for Olofin. He was told to keep plenty of small yams in the house, and to be roasting one for Esu before commencing the day's divination. After making the sacrifice for six days, there remained one yam.

On the morning of the seventh day, Olofin sent a frantic message to him to report at the palace without any delay. Without roasting the last yam for Esu, he left for Olofin's palace, promising to roast it after returning from the palace. When he got to the palace, Olofin told him to make divination to find out why his subjects had paid no homage for quite a while.

After divination, he told Olofin to make sacrifice because on that day, his hunters would report to him that they had shot a; boa constrictor, deer buffalo and an elephant. Olofin quickly made the sacrifice with cock, hen, pigeon and snail. Okpini made the sacrifice after which he returned to his house.

Meanwhile, Esu took position on the main gateway to the town (ubode or ughe) where he began to warn every hunter going to the palace not to go there because some Awos were making sacrifice for Olofin and had ordered that any hunter reporting that he had shot any game on that day, should himself be used for sacrifice. With that warning, all hunters bringing games to the palace and those coming to report what animals they had killed in the forest, stopped at the gate-way for fear of losing their lives.

The people spent the night at Ubode, while Esu retired to spend the night in his own house. The following morning, Olofin sent for Okpini to let him know that his predictions did not come true. That was the time that he gave the last roasted yam to Esu, after a delay of twenty-four hours. Soon after making the sacrifice, he got Olofin's message and left for the palace, where the Oba gave him the length of his tongue as a result of the failure of his predictions to manifest. He felt so thoroughly disgraced because Olofin called him a cheat and a liar.

Okpini was so depressed that he went to the river Oshun to throw in his Ifa before returning home. Meanwhile, after eating the day's roasted yam from Okpini, Esu went back to the hunters waiting at Ubode and gave them the all-clear. He told them that the Awos had completed their sacrifices and that they could all proceed safely to the palace. All of them arrived at the palace simultaneously to report their achievements. When Olofin asked why they were all arriving simultaneously, they explained that on account of the frightful message they got the previous day, they were afraid to enter the palace for fear of being used for sacrifice, sequel to which all of them had to spend the night at Ubode.

Olofin finally realized that Okpini's predictions came true after all, and so sent once more for him. He was just arriving home from the river Oshun when Olofin's messenger arrived. On getting to the palace, Olofin in a conciliatory mood, greeted him with "urukere jenti jenti". He apologized to Okpini for the way he spoke to him the previous day, but asked whether there was a sacrifice he had failed to make. Okpini confirmed that he owed Esu a roasted yam, before he came to the palace the previous day.

Olofin subsequently told him how his predictions eventually manifested albeit after a delay of twenty-four hours. He was given a beaded fly whisk (Urukere) and a goat to atone for his embarrassment. He collected his atonement gifts and returned home. Thereafter, he left for the river Oshun where he retrieved his Ifa units of 5,5,3,2 and it took him a long search for the last one, which he could not retrieve because a fish had swallowed it. He took one pebble from the river to represent the 16th seed and he served the Ifa with the goat given to him by Olofin. That was how this odù earned the sobriquet of Irosun-Okpini.

When this odù appears at divination for a man, he should be told to have his own Ifa. If he already has Ifa, he will be told that he is not serving him faithfully and that he should learn Ifa because he is supposed to practice Ifism. If it appears for a woman, she will be advised to tell her husband to have Ifa, but that if he refuses, he will either be short-lived or she will eventually leave him. If the woman has not got a child, she will be told that she will only have a child after killing three goats for Ifa, or if her husband agrees to have his own Ifa. She has three enemies who are witches and that in her father's village are three trees; Iroko, Oak, and Agbo or Ukhu, There is also an Osan agbalumo tree in the village. A special sacrifice has to be made for her at the foot of those trees by calling the names of the three witches - Aje Umobi, Aje Umosan and Aje Umaghun.

When this odù appears for a pregnant woman or at a naming ceremony divination, the child should be named Awoyemi if a male, and Ifayemi if a female.

Divination for a Barren Woman:

Bi inu ba ti nri, beni obi nyan, were the two awos who made divination for Orunmila and for a barren woman. Orunmila was told to make sacrifice with a hen to Ifa on account of a woman who was coming to marry him. The barren woman called Oshun was also told to make sacrifice with ekure, akara, eko and a pigeon. She was told that she would walk to meet an Ifa priest who was going to be her husband and for whom she would bear children. She was also told that she would find the man on top of a horse (or car in the modern parlance).

As Orunmila was riding on top of his horse one day, he came across a woman who refused to move out of the way for him. The woman explained that life had seized to have any meaning for her and would prefer to be trampled to death by the horse.

When Orunmila dismounted to find out her problem, she cried that she had just come across a hen with its chickens, and a goat with its kids, which made her wonder what she had done to make God deny her the pleasure of having a child.

Òrúnmìlà eventually took her home to make divination for her. When he subsequently made divination for her, Irosun-Okpini appeared.   Orunmila told her that a child was on its way to her. Eventually, she spent the night with Orunmila during which they made love. The following morning, she went home and Orunmila travelled out for Ifa practice. She did not see her menstruation at the end of her monthly cycle. She had become pregnant and in the fullness of time, gave birth to a male child who was named Awoyemi. The birth of the child coincided with Orunmila's return from his tour. They were both happily married ever after.

When it appears for a barren woman, she will be told that unless she moves out of her present home or environment, to marry a physician or doctor, she will not be able to have a child.

The divination made for him before leaving heaven

Chapter **12**

IROSUN-EKA
IROSUN-AYOKA

```
II  I
 I  I
II  II
II  II
```

Made Divination for Esin and Afon:

Ero ma sun l'ara, Ero ma sun l'apa.
Ero ma sun mi Ijesa obokun.
O di'le eleka mogun.
Omo erun ti n ka owo agada le'ri,
Omo erin ti n ti owo ija fon yo.

They made divination for Esin and Afon when they were anxious to have children. Each of them was told to make sacrifice with rabbit, snail and a hen. Afon gave money to Esin to buy the materials for the two of them to make the sacrifice. Esin however only bought materials for herself and proceeded to make her own sacrifice.

She subsequently became pregnant, which condition she succeeded in concealing from her friend, Afon, until she delivered the child. When Afon saw that Esin had a child, she began to cry and blame herself for not going to make sacrifice by herself. Rather belatedly, she went for her own sacrifice with a rabbit, a snail, a he-goat and shea-butter (ori-owo). After making the sacrifice, the Awos prepared medicine for her to be rubbing on her body. At the end of the month, Afon's body began to swell and at the end of 81 days, she began to have children all over her body.

After having her children, Afon told Esin never to allow them to set eyes on each other ever again. That is why to this day, as soon as Esin sees Afon, she will surely fall down.

When this odù appears at divination, the person will be advised to refrain from doing evil. For a spinster, she would be advised to make sacrifice in order to have children after marriage. For a man, he will be told to make sacrifice so that his wife may not have problems in having children. He should be warned not to think or do any evil.

He Made Divination for Ogun:

Oniki Irosun ma sunka, Emina ni ki Irosun maa sunka.
Odunjo alagbede koo kpale Ogun. Adifa fun Ogun omo onijon
o le ni ojo t'on lo fi ara re je olu si oke ire.

Irosun, do not sleep any and every where. The blacksmith did not scrub the house of Ogun at year's end. Those were the names of the Awos who made divination for Ogun when he was going to make himself ruler of Ire. He was told to make sacrifice with a dog and a cock. He made the sacrifice.

When he got to Ire, he met people drinking palm wine and standing gourds of palm wine. Thinking that there was still palm wine in the standing gourds (the usage is to lie empty gourds on their side) he was annoyed when he was not invited to drink from the palm wine. In his state of paranoia, he brought out his sword and slaughtered everyone around. When he later took up the gourds, he saw that they were empty.

When the king heard of Ogun's indiscretion he gave orders for his arrest. A fight ensued in which Ogun fought his way to the palace, killed the king and made himself the new king of Ire. That is why he is called "Ogun Onire agbadamu, Akpaire bi ire do". That is, the one who fought Ire and made himself king over them.

When this odù appears at divination, the person should be advised to be hospitable to his visitors.

He Made Divination for Orunmila To Subdue Death:

Uwo aghoro, emi aghoro, kini she t'oun fowo olima womi lara.

You are a divine priest and I am a divine priest, why did you touch me with unclean hands. That was the name of the Ifa priest who made divination for Òrúnmìlà when he stopped the nuisance effect of Death. Death was ravaging the town at will and the Oba invited Orunmila to do something about it. At divination, he was told to make sacrifice with small chicken (Oromu-adiye) plantain roasted with its skin and roasted corn and to put the sacrifice at the main junction leading to the town.

When Death was returning for a fresh attack, he saw all the things he forbade and the live chicken was shouting uku ye, uku ye, which was a command for Death to take to his heels. He subsequently ran back in fright to heaven, leaving the town in peace.

At divination, the person should be advised to be close to Orunmila so that Ifa might tie up the death that traditionally kills people in his family, so that it might not reach him.

He Made Divination for Eziza To Become Indispensable:

He told Eziza to make sacrifice to his guardian angel and to give he-goat to Esu so that nothing can happen in his community without his presence. He made the sacrifice.

Subsequently, when the Oba of the town wanted to perform an important ceremony, he gave instructions that all divine priests should be invited. When all the invitees were assembled, the Oba told the Awo to begin the ceremony. The Awo however insisted that one divine priest, Eziza was not present. The Oba gave orders for him to be brought in, if necessary by force.

When the messengers got to his farm, they met him eating. When he was told that the Oba wanted him to come to the palace, he replied that he had work to do in his farm. When the messengers wanted to arrest him, he turned into smoke and they could not find him. Later, he resumed eating his food, after which the royal messengers tried a second time to arrest him and he turned into the wind.

When this Ifa appears at Ugbodu, the person will be advised to have his own Eziza and to serve his head with a cock. He should beware of a town-wide meeting or conference, which he should only attend after giving he-goat to Esu. At divination, the person should serve Ogun and Eziza and his head on account of an event that is going to take place in the town.

The Divination Made Before Leaving Heaven:

Okiti kpuke awo eba ono, was the Awo who made divination for Irosun-Ayoka when he was coming to the world. He was advised to make sacrifice to: his guardian angel with a goat, which he was to use to feast the divinities; Esu with a he-goat, Ogun with a dog, cock and tortoise. He was required to make the sacrifice because he was destined to be a prosperous Ifa priest on earth, and that his success was going to evoke animosity against him from fellow Awos and his own relations. He made all the sacrifices before leaving for earth.

He got to the world and began to practice as an Ifa priest. He was so effective that news of his proficiency soon spread to the known world. He was also well known in the courts of the ruling monarchs of his time. He also divined for divinities. Meanwhile, he began to have problems from his household. His wives were not giving him peace of mind and his brothers and sisters had brought his matter to the cult of witchcraft with a view to thwarting his efforts.

While he was wondering what to do about his problems, his guardian angel appeared to him one night to remind him that he had not repeated on earth the sacrifices he made before leaving heaven. Why was he helping everybody else to survive and flourish through sacrifice while he was not making any himself. The following morning, he sounded Okeponrin and his own odù appeared. Ifa told him to; feast his fellow Awos and his brothers and sisters with a goat and a ram, serve Esu with a he-goat and all edible foodstuffs, and to serve Ogun with dog, cock and tortoise. He lost no time in making the sacrifices.

Two days after making the feast, the daughter of one of his brothers cried out from her sleep that she had something to tell Orunmila. The girl would not rest until she got to Orunmila's place where she told him that the problems he was encountering were procured by the cult of witchcraft. She mentioned a number of popular divine priests, two of his wives and practically all his brothers and sisters, including her own father. She disclosed that although the feast he made was well received by the people of the day, he did not extend it to the people of the night. The girl told him that he should make an adequate sacrificial feast to the elders of the night.

He acted in accordance with the advice of the girl by frying a goat, hen and rabbit for the council of the night. Thereafter, two prominent divine priest in the town who were his deadliest enemies died. His brothers and sisters stopped bothering him because the girl's confession was reported to the Olofin who invited all the people mentioned including two of his wives to swear to the divinity of the ground never to bother Orunmila anymore.

The incident enhanced his popularity as an effective Ifa priest, which earned him the sobriquet of Irosun-ala-yoka. He became even more prosperous and his days in Ife were marked by general prosperity, peace and tranquility. The Olofin eventually made him his second-in-command, a position which he enjoyed to a ripe old age.

When this odù appears at Ugbodu, the person will be advised to make the Esu of his Ifa without delay and to have his own Ogun and Eziza shrines. He will be very prosperous in his work, provided he makes the special sacrifices which the odù made on earth. He should expect to have problems from envious co-workers, relations and disgruntled wife or wives during which he should make a feast to all and sundry. His fame and fortune will flourish after making the feast.

When it appears at ordinary divination, the person will be required to have his own Ifa and to serve Esu with a he-goat in order to prosper in his work.

Chapter 13

IROSUN-ETURUKPON

```
II   I
II   I
I    II
II   II
```

He Made Divination for Fire When He Was Coming to Earth:

Bi omode ba mu uwaju owo shi she, aamu eyin owo danu.
odifa fun una omo awo liko orun magbeje.

When a young person works with the front of his hands, he will use the back of his hands to scatter it. That was the name of the Awo who made divination for Fire when he was coming to the world. He was told to make sacrifice with the red clothes he was wearing and red cock, so that his good gestures might be appreciated and aptly rewarded. He did not do the sacrifice.

That is why people neither appreciate nor express gratitude to Fire for all the good work he does for humanity and divinities alike.

When it appears at divination the person will be told to make sacrifice so that his magnanimity might be appreciated and not rewarded with ingratitude.

He Made Divination for Orisa:

Irosun titu a lore. Odifa fun Orisa-turu-yegbe nijo
t'on sun ekun ari leni enimara.

He made divination for Orisa turuyegbe when he was complaining of lack of followership. He was advised to make sacrifice with roasted yam, palm wine, pigeon and cock. He made the sacrifice and after preparing it, he was told to deposit it on the way to his farm. He did so accordingly.

After depositing the sacrifice, he hid to see what was going to happen to it. Ogun, who had been away to war was at that moment returning with three women. One of the women was an albino, the other was a cripple, while the third one had a hunchback. Ogun and his followers were already very hungry. When they saw the sacrifice deposited by Orisa turuyegbe, Ogun thanked whoever made it, and they fed on it, after which they drank the palm wine.

As they were drinking the palm wine, Orisa-turuyegbe came out to accuse Ogun of stealing.

To avoid being summoned before the court of divinities, Ogun surrendered the three women to Orisa-turuyegbe, who took the women home to live with them. They eventually gave birth to children who did not inherit their mothers' deformities. Orisa became very happy and thanked the Ifa priest who made divination and sacrifice for him.

When it appears at divination, the person should be advised to be close to Òrúnmìlà in addition to having his own Ogun and one divinity that drinks no wine. He is likely to get married to three women who will be sent to him by those divinities.

The Divination Made for Him Before Leaving Heaven:

Before leaving heaven, he was told at divination to give a goat to his guardian angel to feast the higher powers and to give a he-goat to Esu, in order to have a successful sojourn on earth, because he was going there rather prematurely. He refused to do the sacrifice.

As he was returning from where he made divination, he met Ogun on the way. When Ogun asked him for food, he replied that he had none to give.

As he was eventually leaving for earth, his guardian angel warned him that he was not going to make it on earth without making sacrifice.

On getting to the world, he built his house near a river and was practicing Ifa art. In the course of his Ifa practice, he met a woman and married her. That was when Esu decided to deal with him. Esu left for his place with a male escort and a gourd of poisoned palm wine, which he kept in his bag. Before getting to Irosun-Tutu's house, Esu stayed behind and told his escort to go to him for divination, while holding the gourd of wine in hand.

When he made divination for the man and his own odù appeared as Ayeo, ostensibly to warn him of the approach of danger, he could not comprehend the significance. Since the tradition is to give Ifa kola and wine as soon as one's odù appears at divination, he began to look for wine to use. The divinee readily obliged by giving him the gourd of wine he was holding in his bag. After pouring libation to his Ifa, he drank out of the palm wine.

As soon as the visitor left his house, he became ill. All the veins in his body went flabby and he became very ill. He ran to so many places to get cured but to no avail. Eventually, he met Ogun who demanded sacrifice with fourteen different animate and inanimate materials. He produced them but was hospitalized in Ogun's house for three years before becoming well. Nonetheless, he lived a life of abject poverty before he died. When he returned to his guardian angel in heaven, he complained that he lived a miserable life on earth. His guardian angel asked him how he could have expected to reap what he did not sow, and that his ignoble experience on earth was the price he had to pay for refusing to make sacrifice be fore leaving heaven.

When this Ifa appears at Ugbodu, the person should be told to prepare his own Ogun shrine in addition to Ifa and Esu in order to have some respite. He is not likely to be exceedingly prosperous in life.

He Made Divination for Kinridin:

Irosun tutu, babalawo Kinridin, odifa fun Kinrindin ni jo
t'on fi omi oju shubere aya tuurutu.

He told Kinridin to make sacrifice with a hen, rat and fish and the skull of a cat. He made the sacrifice and Orunmila prepared a magic belt (akpalode) for him to be wearing.

Meanwhile, there was an outbreak of war in his town and everyone was running helter-skelter. Kinridin suddenly found himself taking refuge in the Oba's palace. He met three other refugees at the palace. One of them asked for drinking water, and he was given water to drink. The second refugee was hungry and begged for food and was fed. On his part, Kinrindin saw a beautiful girl in the palace and asked to be allowed to make love to her even if he had to be killed after the act. He was given a room in which to make love to the girl.

While he was having sex, the royal executioner was invited to get ready to slaughter him for sacrifice to Ogun. Knowing that he was going to be killed after satisfying his sexual urge, he brought out his magic belt and touched the girl with it and she immediately turned into a rat. When he wore the belt once more on his waist, he too turned into a cat. After waiting too long for them to come out, the palace police forced the door open only to discover that they were no where to be found. The cat and the mouse had hidden themselves in the roof of the house.

Meanwhile, an alarm was raised for all the palace guards to watch out for them. Eventually, the cat caught the rat in its mouth and ran away from the palace. After leaving the palace pre-cincts, they transfigured back into human beings and ran to the bank of the river where they met a boat that was about to take off. They hailed on the paddler to pick them up, but he refused. The daughter of the paddler took pity on the man and threatened her father that she would jump into the river if he did not carry the couple. He eventually took them on board and into safety. Kinrindin prospered with his wife ever after.

If it appears at Ugbodu, the person is likely to marry in critical circumstances. He would probably seduce the wife from a stronger person, but will get away with it, if he serves Ifa with four guinea-fowls, Esu with a he-goat, and a war-cock for Ogun.

At divination, the person should serve Esu with a he-goat, and Ogun with a cock. If it appears for a woman, she is likely to leave her first husband to marry a second one.

He Made Divination for Water When His Life Was Hot:

Irosun din din bi eni sada. Be a ko sada. Odu ti o
jade la n ki.

He made divination for the water when his life became very hot. He was advised to make sacrifice with 16 snails and plenty of shea-butter (ori-oyo). He made the sacrifice after which the rain began to fall to cool water down. That is why the approach to the river is generally very cool.

When it appears at divination, the person will be told that his life is not settled. To avoid becoming ill from thinking, he should make sacrifice to Ifa with sixteen snails.

Chapter **14**

IROSUN-OSE
IROSUN-AKPERE
IROSUN-SEKPERE

```
  I   I
 II   I
  I  II
 II  II
```

Ohun kon shosho la aja fo.
Odifa fun Ajibola t'in she ore eleye

It is only one sound that the gong chants. That was the name of the Awo who made divination for Ajibola when she was befriending a witch. Ajibola did not know that the friend was a witch. Each time she became pregnant, it would abort, not knowing that her friend was causing the abortions. Her friend was always watching to know whenever she was pregnant. No sooner would she know then Ajibola would invariably lose the pregnancy.

After losing so many pregnancies in the process, she went to Orunmila for divination. She was advised to make sacrifice with a rabbit, hen and pigeon. After making the sacrifice, she was advised never to meet her friend unless she wore loose apparel to conceal her abdomen. Subsequently she became pregnant without her friend knowing. By the time she knew about it, she could not do anything to it. Ajibola subsequently gave birth to her child, and had many more.

When this odù comes out for a woman, she will be told that she is in her early months of pregnancy, but she will be advised never to visit her friend without wearing clothes to conceal her abdomen, because her friend is a witch, capable of spoiling her pregnancy.

The Divination Made for Him When He Had a Bad Friend:

Yio Sekpere, mi o Sekpere (3 times)
Sekpere ma nkon owo ewu reje. Yio shekpere
mi o Sekpere. Oshe kpere ma okon ubi oje loja la ujo
omo araye. Yio shekpere mi o sekpere. Oshekpere ma oduro
kokoko oje oloja la wujo ikin. Yio oduro oje loja kuwaju ki akun keyin ke ashe tie.

The yam fared well and produced a good tuber. The maize bore fruits, the prince was successful when he inherited his father's crown. The principal Ifa seed (Oduro) fared well to become king of its fellow ikin. After being crowned king he had followers both to his front and to his rear.

This odù has the good fortune of succeeding in whatever he tries his hands, but success will come gradually and not torrentially. He started life by becoming a farmer, and he was always recording prolific harvests.

One day, his friend told him to give up farming and to take to trading. He also prospered as a trader, and excelled his friend who was also trading. Once again in the hope of undoing him, his friend suggested that he should take to hunting. He accepted his friend's advice and his hunting also turned out to be a success story.

Eventually, his friend prepared charms against him, which made him to become ill. When he consulted Ifa, he was told to serve; Esu with a he-goat, and Ogun with a cock, so that Esu would bring a physician who could cure him. He made the sacrifices.

At the time he was trading, there was a regular customer called Odimidimi who used to buy things from him. With a view to buying more wares from him, Odimidimi came to his house not knowing that he had given up trading. When he was told what Odimidimi wanted, he was able to provide them from his old stock.

He did not know that Odimidimi was himself a diviner and physician. When Odimidimi noticed that he was too ill to get up from his bed, he proposed that he would send people to bring him to his house for treatment.

After divination, Odimidimi told him that his bosom friend was the enemy trying to kill him. He made sacrifice for him and prepared medicine for him to bath for seven days. Before the end of the seven days, he became well. Meanwhile, his friend ran away from the town never to be seen again. He became very prosperous eventually.

When this Ifa appears at Ugbodu, the person will be told that he will prosper in any vocation he takes to, because he was destined to succeed in whatever he does. He should serve the new Ifa with a goat, and a hen, give cock to Ogun, and he-goat to Esu. He should however beware of friends. If his instinct tells him to do anything and his friend tell him not to do it, he should go ahead and do it. Without any risk of regret.

If it appears at divination, the person should be told not to be in a hurry to acquire wealth. He will prosper slowly but steadily. One year will always see him prospering more than the previous year. If he does not develop the acquisitive tendency, he will become very wealthy in the end.

Sacrifice for Prosperity:

Orunmila said wonders and I said wonders. He said it was a wonderful year that made Alara to prosper more than the previous year. Last year he wore a simple cap made of cloth, but this year, he is wearing a crown richly woven with beads and beautiful feathers. Orunmila also observed that this year was a better year for Ajero than the previous year. Last year he wore a simple gown, but this year he is wearing a big gown richly embroidered with beads. Orunmila said that the same was true of Orangun of Illa, who walked about on foot the previous year, but was riding on a horse this year.

That is why Orunmila regards this year as a wonderful year. When he was asked for the required sacrifice, he mentioned a big goat, a big rat, and a big fish for serving Ifa so that the new year will bring the person more prosperity than the previous year.

When it appears at divination, the person will be advised to make sacrifice so that next year will find him more prosperous than the current one.

He Made Divination for Paraka, The Masquerade:

Ijan gbajan, Ijagidi jan - were the Awos who made divination for Paraka, the masquerade, when birds were disturbing him from sleeping in the night. He was advised to make sacrifice with a piece of white cloth, an axe, a baton, a cock and a he-goat.

He made the sacrifice, Thereafter, Esu took out a talking drum in the night and played it round Paraka's house and drove away the witches who were holding meetings on the tree out-side his house at night. When the witches heard the beating of the talking drum, which was announcing that Paraka was ready to do battle with an axe on his right hand and a club on his left hand. The witches ran away and did not come anymore to Paraka's house.

When it appears at divination, the person will be informed that witches are disturbing him and that there is an evil bird crying near his house at night. He should make sacrifice to drive the witches away from disturbing his life.

The Divination He Made Before Leaving Heaven:

Kpere Lere mi kpere - was the Awo who made divination for Orunmila when he was coming to the world.

He was told at divination to make sacrifice to his own mind because he was going to have problems on earth which would even make him contemplate taking his life. He was told to serve his mind with guinea-fowl and the middle of a tuber of yam, after cutting off its head and tail. He was also told to serve; his guardian angel with a rat called ukpere in Yorùbá and ebete in Bini and to give he-goat to Esu. He made all the sacrifices, after which his guardian angel forewarned him that life was going to be very problematic for him on earth, but asked him for a set of ayo game equipment (okpan ayo in Yorùbá and ogiurise in Bini). After doing as he was told, his guardian angel assured him that nobody would be able to harm him on earth. He then left for the world emerging in a town called Okegon in Yorùbá land.

He was a responsible man and very well respected Ifa priest. The Oba of Egon grew to like his behavior. Meanwhile, the divinity of Obstacle, to whom he paid no homage before leaving heaven, soon went on his trail. The members of the Oba's household had become very fond of him. While he was at home one day Elenini directed a woman from the Oba's household to visit him. As he was about to make love to her, his guardian angel jerked him into remembering the sacrifice he made to his mind in heaven. He subsequently refrained from making love to the woman. Nonetheless, the woman reported the incident to the Oba, and even lied that he actually made love to her.

The Oba felt so disappointed that he immediately convened a meeting of the town's council of elders. The woman, a wife of the Oba, confirmed the allegation before the council. When he denied the allegation, no one believed him. He was sentenced to be executed after seven days, during which nobody was to visit his house.

He began to weep and all his wives and children deserted him, except for one son who stood by him. While he was weeping, his young son brought out his okpele and threw it on the floor. Since the boy did not know how to read or interpret Ifa, he asked his father to take a look at it. His father declined because he could no longer see it.

Meanwhile, his son remembered the bald-headed Awo who used to visit his father. The boy went to meet the Awo, called kpere kpere ni eku jagho (The rat eats the skin of animals in bits), to tell him that his father having been condemned for an offence he did not commit, was lamenting to death. The Awo followed the boy at once to meet his father. He met him weeping, but when he turned to look at the Ifa on the floor, it was his own odù, Irosun-akpere. He told him to serve Ifa with a guinea-fowl and the middle of a yam tuber, promising to give him a goat if he survived his ordeal. He also told him to serve Esu with a he-goat. The Awo told him that he would be given a chieftaincy title at the end of it all.

That was when he turned to look at the Ifa on the floor, after which he heaved a sigh of relief. He was also told to provide the equipment for Ayo game to his Ifa. He quickly made all the sacrifices. Two days to the day of his execution, Esu visited all the sons of the Oba, the chief and the heavenly police. The children of Oba came to his house to play Ayo game with his son in front of his house. The next chief to the Oba surprised to see the Oba's children playing Ayo with the son of the condemned Orunmila who had been declared persona non grata. The chief immediately went to accuse the Oba of deceiving them into becoming the enemies of Orunmila.

At the same time Esu made one of the children of the Oba to make love to the same woman who lied against Orunmila. At the instigation of Esu, the woman also reported the incident to the Oba. Another council meeting was convened and the woman again appeared to confirm the allegation. The elders observed that since Orunmila had been condemned to death for the same offence, the same fate should apply mutatis mutandis to the son of the Oba.

The Oba refused to pass the death sentence on his own son, but promised to discharge the woman to marry his son. The elders then argued that if the life of the Oba's son was to be spared, the life of Orunmila should also be spared. The Oba readily agreed on the ground, that he was convinced that Orunmila had been falsely accused and that it was his son who had been cohabiting with the woman all along. That was the point at which the woman then confessed that Orunmila did not make love to her.

Eventually, the Oba invited Orunmila to appease him for being falsely accused and wrongly condemned. In addition to giving him a chieftaincy title, the Oba betrothed his eldest daughter to him. Orunmila was amazed at the sudden turn of events. He thanked his son and the Awo who came to his rescue at the darkest of moments. He eventually feasted his Ifa with a goat.

When this Ifa appears at Ugbodu, the person should serve his new Ifa with a guinea-fowl and the middle of a yam tuber, in addition to serving Esu with he-goat to avert the risk of being falsely accused of an offence he did not commit. The person should be advised not to be tempted into making love to his father's wife.

At divination, the person should make the same sacrifice to survive a major test coming to him.

Chapter **15**

IROSUN-OFUN

```
II   I
I    I
II   II
I    II
```

The Divination Made for Him Before Leaving Heaven:

Efun fun Lere - was the Awo who made divination for Orunmila when he was leaving heaven. He was advised not to practice Ifa on earth but to take to trading. He was told to make sacrifice with sixteen pigeons, a goat, a piece of white cloth and 201 cowries to his guardian angel. He was also told to serve Esu with a he-goat, corn, yam, plantain and cocoyam. He made all the sacrifices before leaving for the world.

On getting to the world, he began to practice Ifism, but did not have a settled life. He was otherwise very effective as an Ifa priest, but he did not prosper by it. When he subsequently went for divination, he was told that he had strayed away from the path of his destiny, and that he was supposed to have taken to trading. He was told to serve Ifa by decorating its shrine with white chalk and white cloth. He was told to serve Olókun with a pigeon, a bag of cowries, money, and chalk, and to serve Esu with a he-goat, corn, yam, plantain and cocoyam. He did all the sacrifices.

When Olókun received the sacrifice, he remembered the sacrifice which Irosun-Ofun made to him in heaven and the pledge of support he made to him. Olókun reacted by dispatching his fair-skinned daughter, dressed in white apparel to look for Irosun-Ofun at Oja-ajigbomekon. At the same time, Irosun-Ofun was told to dress in white clothes when going to the market. When Olókun's daughter got to the market, she was the centre of attraction, but spoke to nobody. She was looking for the man dressed in white clothes as her father told her.

Not long afterwards, Irosun-Ofun, also dressed in white, met Olókun's daughter and they fell in love at once. When he introduced himself, she offered to follow him to his house. When she got to his house to see the white decoration and adornment all around, she told him that his house provided a suitable environment for her to stay. He soon discovered that the only food she ate was white chalk, which gave him an idea of who she was.

Meanwhile, the woman advised him to be dressing always in white and to be following her to the market. On every market day, her servants brought wares from heaven to sell on earth, after which she was given the money realized from the sales. On the following market day her servants came with beads, jewels and elephant tusks which were all sent to Orunmila's house. Most of the materials brought by Olókun's servants, had previously not been seen any where on earth. The Oba of the town was subsequently attracted by them and he bought some of them from Orunmila at a price of 200 men and 200 women.

When the other Obas saw the adornments with the Oba of his town, they too, came to buy similar materials from him. He was no treading the path of his destiny and he became exceedingly wealthy. Incidentally, Olókun's daughter had no child for him.

If this odù appears for a light-complexioned man at Ugbodu, he is not likely to prosper and he may not live long, unless he finds a competent Awo who can perform the required special sacrifices (Ono-Ifa of Odife) for him. He will marry a light-skinned woman who will bring prosperity to him. He will undoubtedly do business with foreigners.

When it appears at divination, the person should be told to prepare Olókun shrine for his Ifa and to serve Esu with a he-goat. He should always wear light colored dresses.

He Made Divination for The Barren Daughter of Orisa:

Onigo, Oshorigo, Akolaja, won dafa fun Fekunwe, Okon bi
omo Orisa, nijo t'oun fi omi oju sshubere omo tuurutu.

Those were the three Awos who made divination for fekunwe (one who baths with tears), the only daughter of Orisa, when she was desperately anxious to have a child. They advised her to marry Orunmila (that is, an Ifa man) in order to have a child. She did, and subsequently began to have children.

When it appears at divination for a woman, she will be told to marry an Ifa man and to be serving one divinity in her family, in order to have children, and to settle down in life. If it appears for a man, he should be told to have his own Ifa and to look for a divinity in his family and get initiated into it, and be serving it together with Ifa.

Orunmila Declares God The Only Saviour:

In a dialogue with his followers, Orunmila asked them to name the force and power that can bring joy and satisfaction to one's life. They mentioned the divinities and he declined.When they could not produce an appropriate answer, he declared that it was the Creator and Father of all creation alone that can bring enduring peace and prosperity to his children. When they asked for the sacrifice, he told them to fetch snails, white kola nuts and salt, for offering thanks to God. When it appears at divination, the person will be told to be using chalk and salt to offer prayers and thanks to God as often as he can remember.

He Made Divination for Omonile When He Was Traveling:

Eshin she kere kere, Eshin la ibu are ja; Ipale la nu
ko le so oro.

Those were the three Awos who made divination for Omonile when he was travelling. He was told to make sacrifice with four pigeons, black soap, beads, any seed from a tree, white chalk, animal faeces. He made the sacrifice before embarking on the journey after the Ifa priests had prepared the sacrifice and medicine for him, with which to bathe. He realized a lot of benefits from the journey and he became rich. He then sang in praise of his Ifa priest.

When it appears at divination, the person will be advised that his prosperity will come far away from, the town of his birth. He should provide 2 pigeons in addition to the above materials for Ifa priests to prepare a soap for him to be bathing every Thursday of the week.

Made Sacrifice for Adeyosola:

Ashe gini gbo, Akpa juba ni odan, ogbologbo ara
igbo lo nshe igi to tun fi eyin re ko wa le.
Adafa fun Adeyosola omo eleyin ishawewe t'onfi
gbogbo ara re di kolo winrin winrin, nijo t'oun
fi omi oju shubere omo tuurutu.

The person who goes to fetch fire wood in the forest, the person who goes to fetch materials from an old farm, and the man who stays in the bush and fetches fire wood and carries it home on his head or shoulder, were the names of the Ifa priests who made divination for Adeyosola, the pretty woman with tribal marks all over her body, when she was crying for not having a child. She was advised to make sacrifice with a hen and eight eggs, and to persuade her husband to have his own Ifa. She did as she was told and ended up having five children for her husband.

He Made Divination for The Divine Priest and His Friend:

Ofene-da gharine. A poor man does not enumerate what he forbids. An Orisa priest and his Albino friend became so friendly that to avoid any misunderstanding between them, they told each other what they forbade. The Orisa priest forbade wine and the Albino forbade salt.

One day they both attended a meeting which lasted for so long that everyone became hungry. The Orisa priest excused himself to look for something in the bush. When got to the foot of a tree, he found a gourd of palm wine and he drank out of while, the Albino friend was looking on. As they were returning to the meeting, they were invited to partake in eating a yam porridge prepared with salt. They both ate out of it.

Later, the Albino told the divine priest that he was going to reveal that he saw him drinking palm wine, but the later reminded his friend that he too partook in a meal prepared with salt.

When it appears at Ugbodu, the person should be told that there is someone in his family who is watching to undo him out of envy. He should refrain from drinking wine, and make sacrifice with hen and pigeon. At divination, the person should serve Ifa with hen and snails. If it appears for a woman, she should be told that she has committed adultery, and that unless she confessed the act to her husband, she would not be able to have a child.

IFISM
The Complete
Works of Òrúnmìlà

Volume Nine
The Odus of Owanrin

Chapter **1**

OWANRIN-SO-OGBE

```
 I   II
 I   II
 I    I
 I    I
```

Divination Made for Ogun and Orunmila:

When this odù appears at divination, the diviner should ask for a small quantity of palm oil to drop on the ground before interpreting it.

Esi oun serun de, Erun rin ogoro mudi. Awo
Udi Orisa, udi Orisa oni ehu kangogo. O da mi
lebe moriru. Odami lebo kan le gerete. Odami
lesu itu momesu itu.

Those were the five Awos who made divination for Ogun and Orunmila when they were coming from heaven. God had warned the two of them not to kill any other divinity or human being, because he did not create divinities, mankind and animals to destroy their own species. God made it abundantly clear that anyone who engaged in killing would only be doing so as an agent of Èsù.

Before leaving heaven, they both went for divination and were advised to serve Èsù with a gourd of palm oil, a strong he-goat, and (iso-aparo in Yorùbá, ihuawa in Bini) to make sacrifice with a hen, snails, rat and fish. Ogun, who traditionally looked down on Èsù refused to make sacrifice. Orunmila, whose strength lies in making sacrifice, made it. The Awos made the sacrifice for him, prepared medicine for him to be eating and to mix part of it with soap for him to be bathe with. Ogun and Orunmila both left for earth at the same time.

Meanwhile, Èsù who was not appeased by Ogun was determined to teach the Iron divinity a lesson. He went to Ogun to instigate him into irritability in order to make him react violently to any wrong done to him. It was Èsù who incensed Ogun to become the ferocious divinity that he turned out to be. No sooner was he infuriated by Èsù than he proceeded to kill 200 human beings. Èsù also tried to stimulate Orunmila, but he reminded Èsù of the sacrifice he made to him in heaven, emphasizing that he was sent by God to bring salvation to divinities and human beings alike and not to destroy them. He however gave another he-goat to Èsù. After eating his he-goat, Èsù promised to avenge all wrongs done to him. Orunmila was meanwhile using the medicine prepared for him. The mayhem with which Ogun had become associated made people to run away from him and to be going to Orunmila for salvation.

Meanwhile, Orunmila reminded Ogun of God's injunction forbidding them to kill. Ogun retorted by warning Orunmila to mind his own business, and that if he was not careful, he too would become a victim of his inclination to murder. When Ogun raised his sledge hammer to hit Orunmila, he replied that Ogun was joking because, Ihuawa emits smoke but has no fire; the snail climbs the tree but lacks the teeth to bite it; and that when oil sees fire, it melts at once.

With that incantation, Ogun was humored and he told Orunmila that for a divinity to be feared, he must be violent occasionally. Ogun and Orunmila subsequently became friends.

The Beginning of Vengeance on Earth:

Atete doro oda ke ke re. Agbeyin da, oda gbendu gbendu.
Adifa fun Owanrin, abufun ogbe. Owanrin ti yo ogbe to be.

The first to aggress deals a light blow, while the avenger deals a harder blow. Those were the Awos who made divination for Owanrin and Ogbe when they were going to undo each other, in spite of the fact that they were brothers. They were advised to make sacrifice to avoid becoming victims of mutual deceit. They both failed to make the sacrifice. Owanrin was a salt seller while Ogbe was a kola nut seller. They had their respective stalls in the market.

One day, Owanrin went to the market, while Ogbe remained at home. When Owanrin returned from the market, he asked Ogbe whether he did not see the man he directed to invite him to the market. Ogbe replied that he did not see anybody. Owanrin told Ogbe that some people came to the market to look for roasted kola nuts to buy in large quantity. That was why he sent someone to come and invite him to take advantage of the deal. He went on to add that when Ogbe did not show up at the market, he decided to learn the art of preparing roasted kola nuts with a view to imparting the know-how to him.

Owanrin subsequently advised Ogbe to direct his servants to prepare a Kiln (atibaba in Yorùbá and aka in Bini) for baking the kola nuts. The kiln was quickly prepared and all the kola nuts Ogbe had at home were kept in it and covered up while fire was set below to heat them. All the kola nuts were baked dry before the next market day.

When Ogbe however took the kola nuts to the market, there were no buyers. In fact, people thought that he had gone mentally demented because no one sells or eats roasted kola nuts. Meanwhile, Ogbe's wife cried out on account of the bankruptcy that the ill-advised experiment wrought on them. The husband however told her to keep cool because that was not going to be the end of their lives. Ogbe went home dejected but not deflated.

On getting home, Owanrin asked him how he fared in the market and he lied that he sold out all the roasted kola nuts, and that he realized so much profit that he was already arranging to build a bigger house in which to live. Their relationship continued to smolder on because Ogbe successfully concealed his consternation.

After a long time, Ogbe returned from the market one day to ask Owanrin whether he did not see the salt multiplying technologist, he directed to him from the market. Owanrin replied that he did not see anyone. Ogbe told him that when he failed to show up at the market, he learned the expertise of how to multiply salt in order to impart the knowledge to him. In the first place Ogbe advised him to raise as much money as he could, to buy more salt for a miraculous harvesting operation.

Owanrin borrowed money to buy more salt in addition to the stock he had at home. Thereafter, Ogbe told him to instruct his servants to dig a well and to pour all his stock of salt into it and to cover it up. After five days, he would no longer buy salt for sale, but harvest them from the well. He complied with his brother's proposal without delay. The following day, there was a heavy rain because Ogbe had waited for the emergence of the rainy season before retaliating.

Five days later, Owanrin went to the well to escavate salt only to discover that all the salt had melted away. His wife shouted "Ogbe ma she Owanrin oo". That is, "Ogbe has done in Owanrin". Ogbe's wife told Owanrin's wife to shut up her mouth, asking her whether she was not present when her husband struck them the first blow. A fight ensued between the two families and the quarrel was remitted to Orisa-Nla for adjudication. Orisa-Nla observed that although it was forbidden under God's law to repay wickedness with wickedness, nonetheless, since Owanrin dealt the first blow, he should have expected a heavier blow in return, from Ogbe. That was how the saying began "Owanrin-so-Ogbe, Ogbe-so-Owanrin". That is Ogbe and Owanrin traded wickedness with wickedness.

When this odù appears at divination, the person should be told to beware of doing a bad turn to anyone because the victim would surely retaliate. He should however make sacrifice to make sure that he is neither the victim nor the doer of evil.

The Same Awos Made Divination for Orunmila:

Akoda oro oda ko kekere. Agbeyin da oda gbendu gbendu. Adifa fun Orunmila ni ojo ti onlo si ode Akosi. Ugba olokon adiye ni Orunmila ko lo kosibe.

The aggressor made a light impact, while the avenger dealt a harder blow. They were the two Awos who made divination for Orunmila when he was going to the town of Akosi. He traveled to the place with the 200 fowls he was rearing.

On getting to the town, he released the fowls to move freely about. The town had a divine stretch of bush which was forbidden for non-initiates to enter. One day, Orunmila's fowls strayed into the divine bush (igbo-umale in Yorùbá and ugbo-ebo in Bini). When the people saw the fowls roving into the sacred bush, they reported the incident to the Oba, who gave orders for them to be collected and brought to the palace.

As soon as Orunmila was informed that his fowls had rambled into the sacred bush, in consequence of which they had been seized and sent to the palace at the insistence of the Oba, he went to tender his apology, explaining that as a new arrival to the town, he did not know that the stretch of bush was sacred. He recalled the common adage that "visitors do not recognize sacred forest". The Oba however bluntly refused to release the fowl's to Orunmila, and they were subsequently confiscated.

On getting home, Orunmila sounded Ifa who told him to use a chicken to leave the matter in the hands of Èsù. He remained in the town to practice Ifa art. He soon became known in the town and even the Oba came to realize his importance.

On his part, the Oba had a herd of 201 sheep that were grazing freely in the community under the supervision of four shepherds, two men and two women. One day, as the herd were passing by Orunmila's house, Èsù directed some of the sheep to stray into his sitting room. As the shepherds were driving them out of Orunmila's house, they stumbled on his Ifa shrine and scattered all the ikin on the floor. At the same time, Èsù transfigured into a chief to advise Orunmila to lock the gate to his compound. He subsequently arrested all the sheep and their shepherds on the grounds that it was forbidden to scatter his Ifa seeds (ikin) on the floor.

Meanwhile, the Oba was alerted to the event and he was informed that Orunmila had arrested his sheep and their shepherds. The Oba sent a delegation to appeal to Orunmila to release the flock and their shepherds, but he bluntly refused to do so. At the same time, Èsù in the guise of a visiting chief, went to the Oba to ask him how the issue of Orunmila's fowls which strayed into sacred land was resolved. The Oba replied that he refused to release them to Orunmila. Èsù then replied that the matter of the sheep and their shepherds had to be accordingly resolved mutatis mutandis.

Orunmila seized and sold the entire flock of sheep and married the two female shepherdesses, while keeping the two male shepherds as his domestic servants. Thus, he realized a bigger atonement for his earlier loss.

When it appears at divination for a person who is proposing to travel, he will be told to tolerate and bear whatever wrong is done to him in the place, because he will reap a greater reward in the end.

He Made Divination for The Rabbit:

Owanrin-so-ogbe k'Esu gba - made divination for the rabbit when he stole yams from Èsù's barn. When Orunmila saw plenty of yams in the rabbit's house, he asked where he got them from and he replied that he took them from a farm near his house. Unknown to him, that farm belonged to Èsù. Orunmila advised him that the only way he could minimize the inevitable wrath of Èsù was to have his own Ifa. Orunmila told him that the strategy was to ensure that Èsù ate out of the stolen yams. The rabbit immediately arranged to have his own Ifa.

When Èsù asked Orunmila who was taking Ifa, he replied that it was the rabbit. Èsù warned Orunmila that the rabbit was an ingrate who was bound to repay him with ingratitude.

It was at that stage that Èsù confirmed to Owanrin-so-ogbe that he was aware that the yams they pounded for the rabbit's Ifa ceremony were stolen from his farm, but he cursed that the culprit should be caught in another act of robbery and disgraced. Èsù observed that by stealing from the man who prepared Ifa for him, his curse had manifested on the rabbit. Between Èsù and Owanrin-so-ogbe, the rabbit was condemned to eternal stupidity. That is why he uses his Ifa seeds (ikin or kernels) to block his hole to this day.

When this Ifa appears at Ugbodu, the person will turn out to be ungrateful to his Ifa patron. He should go and steal something to complete his Ifa ceremony and make sacrifice with two hens, two guinea-fowls, kola nuts and cowries, to the new Ifa, in addition to giving he-goat to Èsù.

At divination, the person should serve Èsù with he-goat and Ogun with cock, to avoid being caught for stealing or to forestall the risk of being falsely accused of stealing.

Made Divination for Olofin When He Was Building a New House:

Owanrin-so-ogbe. Boregun awo won lo'ode Egba. Igombu awo
won lo'de Ijesha. Eriki didu, awo won lo'de ilushakun. Adafa
fun Olofin olo mu ole ibudo. Ebo loma ru. Ewure lo ma fi shebo.

The three Awos from Egba, Ijesha and Ilushakun, were the Awos who made divination for Olofin when he was going to acquire land for building a permanent abode. He was advised to make sacrifice with a goat. He did the sacrifice, built the house and lived peacefully in it with his family, to a ripe old age.

If it appears at divination for a person who is going to acquire a plot for building a house, he should be advised to make the same sacrifice.

He Divined Cocoyam When Going To Marry Swamp:

Orisanmi, odifa fun kooko t'onlo she aya akuro. Abufun akiko onlo she oko kooko.
I have a good head, was the name of the Awo who made divination for the cocoyam when she was going to marry the swamp. The same Awo also made divination for the cock when he was going to marry the cocoyam. The cocoyam was told to make sacrifice with a pigeon, while the swamp was told to make sacrifice with a hen and a snail. They made the sacrifices. The cock had been told to make a similar sacrifice but he failed to do it.

Meanwhile, the cocoyam began by going to marry the cock, but soon discovered that the house was too hard for her. She left almost immediately to marry the swamp whose house gave he all the comfort she needed for producing children.

She produced many children for the swamp. When it appears at divination for a person planning to get married, he or she should be told that the marriage would be very successful if sacrifice was made. If it is Uree, the marriage will endure, but if it is Ayeo, it will not last.

When it appears for someone who is behaving stupidly, he should be told that he is being destabilized by Èsù. His only solution is to have his own Ifa before he can think straight and prosper in life.

He Made Divination for The Ijimere (Monkey):

Ore ni ki ri ran.

The truth is always bitter, was the name of the Awo who made divination for Ijimere (monkey) when he went to help Ikoko (lion) who fell into a pit, while Gbon owo po po po, was the Awo who made divination for the tortoise when he went to settle the ensuing rift between them.

Ikoko (lion) had been advised to make sacrifice to avoid falling into a trap prepared by human beings. He refused to make the sacrifice. Ijimere was also advised to make sacrifice to avoid becoming the victim of his own benevolence. He was told to make sacrifice with a cock to his mother's head. He did the sacrifice.

Subsequently, Ijimere was pacing up and down on top of a tree when he heard someone shouting for help from below. When the monkey came down to verify what was happening, he discovered that Ikoko (lion) had been caught in a dugout pit. Ikoko begged him for help, but he declined because he had been warned to beware of losing his life out of magnanimity. Ikoko however promised never to be ungrateful to him. Eventually, Ijimere lowered down his tail for Ikoko to grip, while he held tight to the trunk of a tree.

As soon as Ikoko came out of the hole, he refused to release his grip from the tail of Ijimere. As Ikoko was about to kill Ijimere, the tortoise appeared, dressed in the outfit of a heavenly knight. The tortoise asked Ikoko to state his case first. After narrating his case, he removed his grip from the tail of Ijimere to swing them. As soon as Ikoko released his grip, Ijimere swung himself up to the top of the tree and into freedom.

Once on top of the tree, Ijimere began to sing in praise of Ifa:-

> Ore ni ki ri ra
> Oun ni oju, odifa fun
> Oun Ijimere l'ojo ti yio lo
> Yo Ikoko kuro ni nu ofin.
> Oun gbo riru ebo oun ru.
> Oun gbo eru ai tu kesu oun ru.
> Ko i pe, ko ijina,
> awa ba mi laru segun ebo

Meaning:

> The eyes that witnessed the,
> Bitterness of the truth.
> That was the Awo who,
> Made divination for the monkey,
> When he went to rescue the lion,
> Who had fallen into a pit.
> It was the sacrifice he heard and made,
> That made him to survive the ingratitude
> of his beneficiary.

When it appears at divination, the person will be advised to beware of friends. He should be told however to make sacrifice to avoid becoming the victim of his own magnanimity. He will also be forewarned of an impending dispute over land matters or affecting his job. If he makes the sacrifice, someone will appear at the nick of time to deliver him from the inevitable trouble.

Chapter **2**

OWANRIN-OYEKU
OWANRIN-OLOKUN

```
 ||  ||
 ||  ||
 ||  |
 ||  |
```

The Divination He Made Before Leaving Heaven:

Okiti Kpuke awo eba ono, was the Awo who made divination for this odù when he was coming to the world. He was advised to make sacrifice on account of a contest in which he was going to be involved over a woman. He was advised to serve Èsù with a cock and tortoise. He made the sacrifice before leaving for the world.

There was a beautiful spinster at Ife, who was the daughter of Olokun. Ogun and Sàngó had been making amorous overtures to her when Orunmila discovered her. She fell in love with Orunmila as soon as she met him and he requited the love.

On one occasion when she was escorting Orunmila after paying her a visit, they met Ogun and Sàngó on their way to visit her. Prior to that meeting, none of them knew that the others were courting her. Ogun and Sàngó told her to take leave of Orunmila and return home with them because they were coming to visit her. She refused because she was traveling to Orita-Ijiloko. As they were trying to challenge Orunmila, Èsù intervened by turning Ogun and Sàngó against each other. The two of them began to quarrel over why the other was visiting the woman. As the two of them were fighting, Orunmila quietly walked away with her. She became happily married to Orunmila, and she brought prosperity to him.

When this odù appears at Ugbodu, the person will be told to make sacrifice in order to succeed in winning the love of a woman who will bring fortune to his life.

He Made Divination for the Axe and its Handle:

Owanrin yere ki e kuro mbe, ki a ri Ade loju okan. Odifa
fun Edun, abufun Eru re. Won gbo'gun losi awon igi ti owa
ni oko.

Owanrin, make way so that the crown might be visible on the tray. That was the name of the Awo who made divination for the Axe and its handle when they were going to wage war on the trees in the forest. They were both told to make sacrifice with a he-goat. The Axe made the sacrifice but the handle was not interested in making any sacrifice. They were to make the sacrifice in order to survive and return home safely.

They both left for the battle and started combat. After a hard struggle, the handle was killed, got broken and discarded. It was the Axe alone that survived the battle and returned home safely after felling the trees.

When this odù appears at divination for a person who is proposing to travel, he or she will be advised to make sacrifice in order to avoid injury or accident from a dispute in which he is bound to be involved, during the tour. He is likely to be traveling with another person. They should both make sacrifice in order to return home unscathed.

The Divination He Made Before Going To Divine for Olofin:

As a royal diviner, he used to make divination for himself every morning before going to the palace. At one of such daily divinations, Ifa told him to serve his head with a pigeon before going to the palace, and to wear a male skirt (buluku) instead of trousers to the palace. He performed the sacrifice and dressed in buluku for the palace.

On getting to the palace, he made the day's divination for the Oba, advising him to make sacrifice with pigeon, guinea-fowl, crocodile and a cow. Olofin told him to come and make the sacrifice the following day. On his way back from the palace, he stopped at a friend's place, and told him that he was going to make a major sacrifice at the palace the following day. He told the friend that the sacrifice was going to involve the slaughtering of a cow.

After leaving for his house, his friend made a public announcement that there was going to be a feast at the Oba's palace the following day. The following morning an unusually large crowd assembled at the palace. When the palace attendants asked the uninvited guests what their business was at the palace, they explained that they had been invited to come for a feast at the palace.

Meanwhile, Owanrin-Oyeku made his morning divination and Ifa told him that in spite of his appointment with the Olofin, he should desist from going to the palace on that day. Accordingly, he stayed home for the whole of that day. He was however told to dub the skull of a he-goat with palm oil and to serve Èsù with it. He did so. Towards evening of that day, Olofin sent a messenger to inform him that he had been expecting him throughout the day. He sent a reply to explain that he was suddenly taken ill the previous night, as a result of which he could not show up at the palace. Thereafter, the Oba gave instructions for the uninvited guests to be fed and detained overnight. When Owanrin-Oyeku came to make his sacrifice the following morning, the Oba drew his attention to the guests he directed to come to the palace for a feast the previous day. He totally denied any knowledge of the matter, and the people confirmed that it was not Orunmila that invited them. The sacrifice was made in earnest and the men were told to return to their homes.

When this Ifa appears at Ugbodu, the person should be advised not to escort or accompany anyone to any ceremony. He should serve Ifa with a crocodile. At divination, the person should be told to serve Èsù with a he-goat to avoid any obstacle, embarrassment or disgrace in the place he is going to go.

The Divination Made for Olofin When He Was Critically Ill:

Owanrin sun lo ye. Sigo sigo agutan. Adifa fun Olofin ni
jo t'onshe ogbogbo arun ni'le t'in roju ati dide.

Sigo sigo agutan was the Awo who made divination for Olofin when he was so ill that he thought he was not going to be able to get up anymore. He was told that he would get up if he made sacrifice with a sheep and all available edible foodstuffs. He made the sacrifice after which he became well.

At divination for a sick person, he should be told to make sacrifice with a sheep. Parts of the sheep should be extracted and offered as sacrifice to the elders of the night, because they will alleviate the illness.

Orunmila's Eulogy of Caution:

Orunmila advises caution in earning and spending money, not to be flirtatious, and to bear the number of children one can conveniently look after.

He added that the person for whom this Ifa appears at Ugbodu should be prudent, judicious and discreet in whatever he does in life. A special sacrifice should be prepared for him with the appropriate leaves of this odù and a frog, in addition to serving Ifa faithfully.

Divination for Heaven and Earth:

Iwon eku ni iwon ite, ki ada'so kan'le
Ki a ma gun ju eni nio fi nye'ni. These were the three Awos who made divination for heaven and earth when God was going to apportion the wisdom of rights and responsibilities to them. The earth was told to make sacrifice with plenty of snails, thick white cloth, white pigeon and a big he-goat. On the other hand, heaven was told to make sacrifice with white cloth, 20 needles, and a big ram. The two of them made the sacrifices after which God gave equal share of wisdom to them, but told them to refrain from doing evil in order to withstand the machinations of Èsù. He proclaimed that there was to be free movement between the two of them.

When this odù appears at divination, the person will be told that he is going to be given a major assignment, or a responsible position. He will be equal to the task, provided he proceeds to make sacrifice. He will never lack the good things in life.

Chapter **3**

OWANRIN-IWORI

```
II  II
 I  II
 I   I
II   I
```

He Made Divination In Heaven for The Queen of Fays:

Atiro gomugo lori lo. Emi mo beje leyin orun.
Adifa fun Amure Nana, omo ataro diri gomugo re ile oko.

These were the two Awos who made divination for Amure Nana, the queen of fays when she was coming from heaven. When they told her to make sacrifice for a long stay on earth, she considered it unnecessary because she intended to return very quickly from the earth, anyway. She instructed her heavenly husband and her followers to wait for her to return to heaven on the day she would be given away in marriage to an earthly husband.

On getting to the world, her parents were warned at her naming ceremony divination that the child was a fay and that the only way of impelling her to live on earth to a ripe old age was for them to betroth her to an Ifa priest without collecting any dowry on her.

When she was ripe for marriage, a day was appointed for Orunmila to take her to his house as his wife. As soon as the date was fixed, her followers, led by her heavenly husband, stood on the way to Orunmila's house ready to return with her to heaven.

Meanwhile, Orunmila sounded Ifa, who advised him to hurry quickly to tell her parents to loosen the hairdo she had just plaited on her head for the occasion. All female fays have a tradition of plaiting their hairdo vertically to point upwards as a mark of mutual identification. When Orunmila got to her parent's house he told them to re-plait her hairdo to be horizontally flat on her head.

When the day came for escorting her to Orunmila's house, her heavenly associates who were waiting for her, could not recognize her on account of the change in her hairstyle. She was led safely to Orunmila's house and lived happily with him ever after.

When this odù appears for a woman at divination, it will be obviously clear that she is a fay. She should be advised to marry an Ifa man if she wants to live long on earth. If she is already married, her husband should be advised to ask the Ifa priest to perform the special sacrifice for tying down fays on the shrine of Èsù.

He Made Divination for The Maize:

Owanrin were rerere, Owanrin weerererere, babalawo agbado
odifa fun agbado. Ani ki agbado rubo ko ba le bi omo.

He made divination for the maize when she was going to the farm to start bearing children. She was advised to make sacrifice with rat, fish, akara, eko, white cloth, white hen and needle. She did the sacrifice. She was told to make a second sacrifice so that enemies may not eat up her children, after bearing them.

On getting to the farm, she brought out the needle first. She produced hundreds of children at a time. But she had failed to make the second sacrifice for protecting her children from being ravaged by human beings, birds, and animals. Èsù soon alerted mankind, birds and animals to the nutrient value of the corn's children. When she found mankind enjoying her children fresh, instead of hurrying to do the second sacrifice, she decided to use her own contrivance to dry up her children, thus making them too brittle for people to eat.

Èsù again advised human beings to pluck her children from the comb and put them in salt water and to fry them subsequently. The comb of the children was used to fry them on the hot frying pan, and it was then she remembered the second sacrifice she did not make. As the children were being fried on the pan, she cried Owanrin wererere, Owanrin wererere - which is the noise the corn makes when being fried for preparation into ekate or uloka.

When it appears at divination, the person will be advised not only to make sacrifice to have children, but also to make a second sacrifice so that enemies may not destroy his/her children after producing them.

The Divination Made for Three Brothers:

Owanrin Iwori ugbo kan ko gba erin.
Eluju kon ko gba Efan.
Won iba ri bi to shy okuku - won iba sa si.
Adifa fun omo shegita she awo,
Atun bu fun omo lakpinla shoro,
Won tu da fun Alaaro wo.
Ani ki awon meteta ru ebo.
Alaaro wo ni kon lo ru ebo.
Ago eyele lo fi ru bo.

These are the names of the three Awos who made divination for three brothers: One was fetching fire wood for sale; the second was splitting fire wood for a living; while third was the one who was treasuring their belongings. Each of them was advised to make sacrifice with a basket of pigeons in order to prosper. Alaaro wo, the third one, who used to treasure his assets, made the sacrifice. He was also the one who prospered, because he used to sell his wares in a shop. He started the practice of displaying wares in a shop or store for sale.

When this Ifa appears at Ugbodu, the person should be advised not to take any profession that involves wood or planks. He should take to trading and make a special sacrifice with 10 pigeons kept in a basket.

The Divination Made for Him When He Was Traveling To Shigo:

Kia asha sha sha, kia shu ni shikutu. Adafa fun Orunmila baba
shawo lo si ilu Sigo.

To butcher it many times, and to tie it up again, are the names of the two Awos who made divination for Orunmila when he was going to the town of Shigo. He was told to make sacrifice and he did.

On getting to Shigo, he did not meet the elders at home. They were all away to their farms. The youths at home told him to wait for the elders, but he asked them whether they at home did not know how to make divination. All the youths came together and he told them to make sacrifice with a sheep. They all joined hands to fund the cost of buying the sheep.

Thereafter, without slaughtering the sheep, he went home with it. Not long afterwards, he left the town and the elders returned from their farms. The youths told them what had happened in their absence. The elders queried who authorized them to make sacrifice. When they told them it was Orunmila and that he went away with the sheep, the elders ordered them to go and retrieve it from him. Try as they ran to catch up with him, they could not reach him. They had to return home without the sheep.

When it appears as Ayeo at divination, the person will be told that he is thinking of getting back what he or she gave to someone, but that he or she will not be able to get it back.

The Divination He Made When His Wife Was Unfaithful:

When his wife was having a secret lover, he did not know, but people who observed her movements came to tell him. When he consulted Ifa, it confirmed that his wife was truly misbehaving, but that he should serve Ifa with a hen so that she might be exposed. He made the sacrifice.

Soon afterwards, his wife began to emaciate and she subsequently became very ill. He was subsequently visited by a Sàngó, priest, and an Ogun priest, who warned the wife that unless she confessed what she did, she would surely die, because Ifa had taken umbrage to her misdeed. The woman instantly confessed her misbehavior and she was told to buy a ram with her own money to appease Ifa. She went to her parents to give her the money and the appeasement was done. She eventually became well.

When it appears at Ugbodu, the man will be told that his wife is flirting. He should give a hen to Ifa and he-goat to Èsù so that she might be exposed.

When it appears at divination, the person should serve his head with a cock so that the actions of a woman might not create difficulties for him.

He Made Divination for The Rat, the Fish and The Snail:

Mowo iwaju, Mowo eyin, were the Awos who made divination for the rat, the fish and the snail. They asked the rat why he was in the habit of stopping to look backwards when he moved. He explained that the death that killed his parents came from the rear. He was advised to make sacrifice to avoid death in a similar manner. He was told to serve Ogun and Èsù and he made the sacrifice. Thereafter he was told to stop looking backwards and the death from the rear did not affect him.

The fish was also asked why he was always looking forward in the water. He explained that the demise of his ancestors was brought about by frontal attacks. He too was told to make sacrifice to Ogun and Èsù and to stop looking forward. He refused to do the sacrifice. That is why the fish is often caught by frontal attacks either by hooks or by nets.

The snail was also told to make sacrifice with chicken to avoid death from the rear. He too did not make the sacrifice. Before then, people used to be afraid of the two swords that the snail has in front of it. For failing to make sacrifice, Èsù told human beings and animals that those swords were totally harmless and that the snail was in fact a coward, who would withdraw the swords to their cases as soon as he was challenged. He however advised that since the snail was defenseless on its back, they could always apprehend him through the back.

When this odù appears at divination, the person will be told that enemies are after him, but that if he makes sacrifice with cock to Ogun and he-goat to Èsù, they will not be able to do anything to him.

The person should be told as well that for failing to attack him, his enemies would direct their attention to his children. He should not undertake the tour he is contemplating so that his enemies might not attack his children in his absence.

Special Sacrifice for Owanrin-Iwori

Orunmila says that sacrifices should be made for the following objectives:

> Pigeon for sacrifice to have money;
> Cock for sacrifice to get married;
> Rabbit for sacrifice to have children;
> Ram for sacrifice to have a higher position;
> Pig for sacrifice to prosper generally; and
> Sheep for sacrifice to live to a ripe old age.

When this odù appears at divination, the Ifa priest will make a special sacrifice for the person, so that his children might be prosperous, famous and be around him at old age and to be with him when he dies. The special sacrifice is prepared with he-goat, the leaves of a tree called Oshe, the leaves of maize, and the leaves of a tree called Akpa. The preparation is ground with the blood of the he-goat and mounted on the skull of the he-goat.

Chapter 4

OWANRIN-SI-IDI
OWANRIN-SIDIN

```
 I   II
 II  II
 II   I
 I    I
```

He Made Divination for The Mushroom:

Owanrin-sidin, kokoro sidin, wonyin. Awon meteta
lo'ndi fa fun Olu-oron, to'ntori omo bo'fa .Ebo ni ko ru o.

These were the three Awos who made divination for the Mushroom (Olu-oron) to have 201 children, but not to keep them. She was advised to make sacrifice with a piece of white cloth and rabbit in order to have children. She was also told to make a second sacrifice so that after having children, they might grow up to become adults before her eyes.

She made the sacrifice to bear children and she had many of them, but failed to make sacrifice to see the children outlive her. On account of the second sacrifice she failed to make, her children did not live for more than 48 hours after being born.

They also made divination for the fly to have children and to live to see her children survive to make her proud of them. She made the sacrifice to have children, but not the second sacrifice to witness their success in life. As soon as the fly gives birth to her many children, before they begin flying, she would die, which is why flies do not have mothers.

When it appears at divination, the person will be advised to make sacrifice in order to witness the survival and prosperity of his or her children. The sacrifice is made with a sheep and a piece of white cloth. The sacrifice is prepared by adding gravel to the head of the sheep, together with the appropriate Ifa leaves and the Iyerosun of this odù on the white cloth and tied up. The wrapped parcel is then given to the person to bury on the floor of his own house. The spot on which it is buried will be prepared with cement blocks in such a way that the person can sit on it from time to time. Thereafter all his children will grow to become prosperous before his own eyes.

The Divination Made for Him When He Went To Elepin-pin:

Lagbo-n-gbo-igi, Lagbo-n-gbo-igi, Akula igi mole gbara-gbara- were the three Awos who made divination for Orunmila when he was traveling for Ifa practice to the town of Elepin-pin. He was also advised to make sacrifice so that enemies would not prevent him from coming home with the gifts he was going to receive in the place. He was told to make sacrifice with a bird called (eye-oge), in addition to water and sand taken from a gutter drain. He made the sacrifice.

On getting to the town, he made divination and sacrifice for several people, who derived satisfaction from his services. He realized several gifts and rewards.

Meanwhile, three girls, who came to him for divination told him that they were only prepared to marry the man who succeeded in knowing their names. He made divination for them, and sang a poem to them:

Agbenu aro Isan
Ijokun tiriki ewa
Agbenu adinmu pin pin pin

were the three fays who left heaven in search of husbands on earth. They had been told that they were the wives of Orunmila and that he would travel to meet them in their place.

As soon as he mentioned the names of the three fays, they all went on their knees to hail him as their husband, because he was the first man to mention their names.

Several suitors had previously approached them for marriage, but they could not know their names.

When those who were interested in the girls heard that all three of them had agreed to marry the visiting Ifa priest, they were determined to stop him from leaving the town with them. When he sounded Ifa the following morning he was told to leave for home furtively that night. Before the conspirators could firm up their disruptive plans, Orunmila was already back home with the three girls and his gifts.

When it appears at divination, the person should be advised to make sacrifice before embarking on a proposed journey in order that the fortune he would obtain in the place would reach home safely with him.

He Made Divination for The Eta and Pepper:

Owanrin mi shiden, Awo eta, odifa fun eta. Abufun Ata ro do.

He made divination for an animal called (eta in Yorùbá and edi in Bini), who was told to make sacrifice with a melon sauce called iru in Yorùbá and evbarhie in Bini) so that his anus might not be emitting an offensive odor. He did not bother to make the sacrifice.

The Pepper (Ata) was also told to make sacrifice to avoid losing her children to enemies. She was told to make sacrifice with the red apparel she was habitually wearing. She did not make the sacrifice because the garment was too precious for her to part with. When Ighoroko told Èsù that Eta and Ata refused to make sacrifice, Èsù punished them by, inserting the Iru or Evbarhie sauce into the anus of Eta, which made his anus o be smelling, while cladding the body of Ata's children with red cloth.

Thereafter, it was the heavy smell of Eta's anus that began to alert his enemies (bigger animals and hunters to her presence wherever he was, which remains her undoing to this day. On the part of Ata, the pepper, as soon as the children wore the red apparel, Èsù told human beings and birds that they were palatable spices for eating and seasoning. Her children subsequently became staple seasoning spices for mankind and food for the birds.

When it appears at divination for a woman, she will be told to make sacrifice so that she does not develop a disease on her genitals, which will not only make her repugnant to men, but also make it impossible for men to have sex with her.

If it appears for a man, he will be told to make sacrifice to avoid contacting carnal disease from a woman. In either case, the sacrifice should be made to avoid losing children.

The Price of Deriding Orunmila as Ordinary Palm Kernels:

Elerin moro aran. Orangun maaja loko. Owa lo mo asonda aaje igbin. Adifa fun egberin aworo t'om bu ikin lo'okuro. Ifa aakpa gbogbo won je.

Those were the Awos who made divination for 800 divine priests when they scoffed Orunmila as a mere palm kernel. He warned them that he would not hesitate to destroy anyone who derided him because that is the only occasion in which he destroys irreparably.

When it appears at divination, the person should be warned not to ridicule anyone disparagingly, to avoid sudden death.

Divined for Orunmila When He Won Respect From Divine Priests:

Owanrin omi ishi den. Iden mi'shu ileke. Adifa fun Orunmila baba lo gba iba ati ashe ni owo alaworo gbogbo. Owanrin discharged worms, and worms discharged beads, were the two Awos who made divination for Orunmila when he was to command the honor of all divine priests.

He made sacrifice with a goat. That is why divine priests give honor and respect to Orunmila in order to become successful.

When it appears at divination, the person will be told to make sacrifice in order to command the honor and respect of his colleagues.

The Feat He Performed, When He Was an Adolescent:

When he was young, he was indentured to an elderly Ifa priest as a servant. One day, he was sent to fetch fire flames from a neighboring house for them to make fire as was the custom at the time. Incidentally, he went to the house of the Olowo, the king of Owo.

As he was going for the fire flames, he passed through the courtyard where Babalawos were divining for the Olowo. When he sighted the odù that was being translated on the Ifa tray, he begged for permission to drop a hint. The Babalawos hushed him down with the adage that it is forbidden for a young person to open his mouth to speak in the midst of elders. The Olowo however prevailed on the Babalawos to give the young boy an audience with the adage that intelligence is never the exclusive monopoly of the elderly.

The boy was subsequently granted audience and he dropped a bombshell by saying that the Ifa on the tray was advising the Olowo to make urgent sacrifice to Èsù with a gun in its case, a cutlass and a hunter's bag, in order to forestall the risk of getting lost, and he added that the Oba should not venture outside the palace for the rest of that day. The Babalawos accused the boy of "blasphemy" on the ground that he did not know what he was talking about. He was instantly told to get lost. He fetched his fire flames and returned to his house.

While the Ifa priests were still battling with the interpretation of the odù, the Oba excused him self to answer nature's call at the back of the house. While he was urinating, he sighted a monkey on top of a tree and he quickly went inside the house to fetch his gun. In his determination to shoot the monkey, he strayed far into the forest until he eventually lost his way. Try as he did, he could not find his way back home. He remained in the forest for three days.

On the third day, Èsù appeared to him in the guise of the young boy who interrupted his divination, and asked him what he would do for him if he showed him the way home. The Olowo promised to betroth his daughter to him. Èsù then led Olowo to the back of his house and disap-peared.

The whole of Owo had been agog for the return of the Oba during the three days. They were relieved when they saw him on the third day. As soon as he got home, he invited Owanrin-si-di, the young Awo to make the sacrifice he had prescribed. After making the sacrifice, the Oba betrothed his daughter called Kakunrin to the young man. The princess had three children for Owanrin-si-di. Meanwhile, the Oba decreed that the people of Owo should be forever forbidden to eat the meat of monkey.

When this Ifa appears at Ugbodu, the person should immediately make sacrifice with a gun and its case, a cutlass, hunter's bag and he-goat to Èsù, so that some tragic event might not prevent him from completing the initiation ceremony.

At divination, the person should serve Èsù with a wooden gun, a cutlass and a he-goat, to avert the risk of being arrested and detained.

Chapter **5**

OWANRIN-OBARA
OWANRIN-KPALABA
OWANRIN-KPAJIBASUDE
OWANRIN-OLOBA

```
 I   II
II   II
II    I
II    I
```

He Made Divination for Palm Wine and The Cooking Pot:

Owanrin bala bala, babalawo Emu, odifa fun emu.
Abu fun Isa.

He made divination for palm wine and the cooking pot. The palm wine (emu) was told to make sacrifice with soap, feathers (iye) and white pigeon. He made the sacrifice. On his part, the cooking pot was told to make sacrifice with a bundle of fire wood, a he-goat and plenty of water. He did not make the sacrifice.

When Èsù was told that Emu made the sacrifice he used his ASE to proclaim that Emu would eternally become indispensable whenever good things were being done, and that anyone who over-labored him would always become tipsy. That is why to this day, wine and spirits abound at all festive occasions, and why those who consume them in excess often get drunk and become intoxicated.

On the other hand, Èsù turned to Isa, the pot, cursing him that for failing to make sacrifice, he would always be forced to do his work under hell fire. That is why fire is made to heat the pot before he is able to cook anything.

When it appears at divination, the person will be told to make sacrifice to avoid unpleasantness in his life, and to enjoy honor and respect in his community.

He Made Divination for The Tortoise:

Owanrin kpalaba ikpabo. Odifa fun Oloba aghun.

He made divination for the tortoise when he was indebted. The lender was often coming to his house to harass him when he could not repay the debt. After divination, he was told to make sacrifice, but since he invariably prefers to rely on his wits, he did not make the sacrifice.

Meanwhile, he told his wife to use him as a grinder anytime the debtor came to demand payment, after telling him that he was not at home. Not long after that, the lender came to his house and the wife lied that he had travelled. At the same time, the wife took him up and used his back to grind corn gradually.

The lender waited sometime, after which he felt insulted because the tortoise's wife was continuing to grind corn without paying any attention to him. The man took the grinder from her and threw it into the surrounding bush. Without realizing that it was his debtor he threw away, the wife aprehended the lender and accused him of throwing away the stone which fetched her money. Meanwhile, the tortoise moved away and concealed himself in an opaque thicket.

The tortoise's wife refused to release her grip on the lender unless he retrieved her grinding stone. The scuffle attracted the neighbors, who told him to go out in search of the woman's grinding stone.

He combed the entire bush without finding it. The interveners subsequently asked him to pay her an amount higher than the debt for which he came to demand payment. Since he did not have that kind of money on him, he excused himself to go home and bring it.

He neither showed up again, nor returned to draw his own debt. That was how the tortoise's indebtedness lapsed.

When it appears at divination, the person will be advised to make sacrifice so that any debt he owes will be written off as bad debt. If someone owes him, he should be advised not to demand the debt with anger, lest it would remain unpaid.

He Made Divination for Ola, Who Dispenses Prosperity:

Owanrin kpalaba awo eti omi. Obara, awo oke odo.
Adifa fun akpakpa oniran iran. Iran ile wa otidi igbo owo.
Iran ile wa otidi igbo aya. Iran ile wa otidi igbeo omo.

Owanrin was the Awo who lived at the bank of the river.
Obara was the Awo who lived on top of the hill over looking
the river.

They Made Divination for Ola, The Divinity of Wealth

The wealth he shared to people enabled them to have money, get married, have children, and build houses. To achieve the good things of life, they were required to make sacrifice with a sheep.

When it appears at divination for a man who is relatively poor, he will be advised to make sacrifice with a sheep because he will surely become wealthy and prosperous, provided he takes his own Ifa.

If it appears for a woman, she will be told that she will have plenty of children and will not be in want for the wherewithal for taking care of them, provided she can make sacrifice.

The Divination Made for Him Before He Left Heaven:

Ule Obara oro ro.
The house of Obara is full of secrets, was the name of the Awo who made divination for this odù when he was coming to the world. He was told to serve; Èsù with a small he-goat to be split on the shrine of Èsù, and the ground divinity with tortoise, snail, cocoyam, corn, plantain, cowries and a gourd of palm oil. The tortoise was to be buried alive in the ground. He was also to serve Ogun and Osanyin with a tortoise respectively. After making all the sacrifices, he left for the world and emerged at the town of Obaa in Ondo State of Nigeria.

On getting to the world, he became a diviner but people began to cheat and deceive him. Wondering why he was not getting on so well, he went for divination and was told to repeat the sacrifice he made in heaven. Once again, he made all the sacrifices. Thereafter, Èsù carried out an advertising campaign in his favor and effectively published his proficiency as an Ifa priest. His predictions and sacrifices began to manifest so effectively that so many people began to seek salvation through him. His fame eventually brought him in contact with the king of Obaa, who appealed to him to assist him in administering the town. He became very famous and prosperous.

The Oba began by telling him about his own problems. The Oba was rather aggressive and dictatorial which deprived him of the cooperation of his people. He also had no children in spite of the many wives he had in his harem. When Owanrin-Obara made divination for him, he advised the Oba to turn a new leaf and extend the hand of fellowship to his people in order to win their cooperation. He was to begin by throwing a feast for his entire people with a cow and a goat, after giving a strong three-year old he-goat to Èsù.

After serving Èsù, the Oba lost no time in making the feast which provided plenty of food and drinks for all and sundry. The feast was well attended because it was a surprise packet to his subjects, having already gotten used to being cold-shouldered by the Oba. After wining and dining, the entire people joined hands in praying for him.

That night Orunmila got parts of the meat and the leftovers of the food for the feast and used them for preparing a big sacrifice for the Elders of the Night. At a subsequent meeting of the club of witchcrafts, they accepted his sacrifice and resolved to untie all the knots they had previously fastened against him.

The change in fortune for him began, when his people resumed the payment of homage to him. The following month several wives became pregnant. Instead of expressing gratitude to Owanrin-Obara, he began to show disrespect to him. One of the Oba's pages, called Ajiba, who challenged him for being so contemptuous to the benefactor who altered his course of his life, was summarily executed on the orders of the Oba. Incidentally, Ajiba had been very friendly with Owanrin-Obara. When the latter heard how his friend was summarily executed because of him, he went to confront the Oba. The Oba retorted by ordering him never to enter the palace anymore and that for being an Ifa priest, he would have made him to suffer the fate of Ajiba. The Oba was taken ill a week later and died suddenly in his sleep without attaining old age.

When this Ifa appears at Ugbodu, the person should be told to forbid eating the meat of tortoise. He should be warned never to show disrespect or ingratitude to his patron who prepared Ifa for him because if he offends him, he would die. At divination, the person should be advised to be bonhomie to his people and community and to prepare a feast for members of his family, so that his problems might be alleviated.

He Made Divination for Tella:

He made divination for a man called Tella when he was too poor to afford the cost of making sacrifice. He was advised to serve his head with 10 bitter kolas and 2 cocks in order to be free from the bondage in which he was. He was working as an indentured bondsman (iwota in Yorùbá and imu in Bini) on account of a debt he could not pay. He could not afford to make sacrifice. He was however able to serve his head with one bitter kola, promising to make the sacrifice in full as soon as he completed his indentured bondage. His wife was pregnant at the time. Meanwhile, it was the yam planting season and Tella went to his creditor's to dig ridges for cultivating seed yams. While digging a ridge, his hoe struck an object which turned out to be a coffin of hidden treasure. He became so exicted he went home singing:

Tella Roko ti ri Owo loko.

His neighbor who overhead him immediately went to report the incident to the Oba who confiscated the find from him on the ground that whatever treasure is discovered anywhere beneath the ground belongs to the king. He was only given the equivalent of fifty pence with which he however made his long delayed sacrifice. After making the sacrifice, he discovered an even greater treasure the next day.

This time, Tella quickly covered up the treasure box and proceeded to complete his ridge digging. Before closing from work on that day, he saw a bitter-kola tree in the bush where he was resting and plucked some of the fruits which were ripe. On his way home, he began to sing:

Mo ri orogbo loko, Tella roko -
I have found bitter kola on the farm.

When the owner of the farm heard him singing he came out to ask him what he had found this time, and he explained that he saw a bitter kola tree on the periphery of the farm and showed him the fruits he plucked from the tree. The man ignored him and returned home.

After dusk, Tella returned stealthily to the farm to collect his new treasure find to his house without even telling his wife. He waited for three days to elapse before he went to his lender to repay his debt of 26 bags of money (egberin dogbon), thus buying back his freedom. Meanwhile, he spent the next three days plucking and selling the fruits of the bitter kola he had discovered near the farm. His master presumed that he repaid his debt from the proceeds of the bitter kola sales. He subsequently became a rich man, and went to thank Orunmila.

When this Ifa appears at Ugbodu, the person should forbid bitter things including vegetables and fruits, beginning with bitter-kola. He should serve his head with 2 cocks while backing his Ifa shrine. He should also provide a hoe to be kept at his Ifa shrine. He should serve Èsù with he-goat.

He should be reassured that although he had previously not been able to make ends meet, Ifa would soon bring prosperity to him.

At divination, the person should serve; Ogun with a cock, and his head with a pigeon and white kola nuts so that he might achieve his ambition in life.

He Made Divination for Olubi To Survive a War:

When Olubi was going to war, he went to Orunmila for divination and he was told to make sacrifice with a cock, the bone of a horse, the leaves of Igi iyeye and sheer butter (ori-oyo). The sacrifice was made by burning the materials and putting the black powder in the shea butter or pomade for him to be rubbing his body every morning.

When the Ifa priest was preparing the sacrifice he repeated the following incantation:

Isun sile ki pa esin.
Isun sile ki pa igi-iyeye
Iyeye ki sun si'le ku-u.
Ereke ni mo ma sun.
Ereke ni mo ma ji-i.

Meaning:

The horse never dies from sleeping on the floor.
Iyeye tree never dies from sleeping on the ground.
Merrily shall I sleep and cheerfully shall I wake.

Olubi went to war and returned victoriously with plenty of loot.

When it appears at divination, the person will be told to make sacrifice to survive an epidemic or a general strife.

When this odu appears at divination, the person will be advised to make prescribed sacrifices to avert the danger of the sudden death of his wife. If it appears for a woman, she will be warned not to take undue advantage of her husband's love to demand favors fraught with fatal consequences for herself and her husband.

This Odu's Special Sacrifice for Prosperity:

Orunmila declared that the corridor of his Father's (God's) house was lined with prosperity. His followers asked him what to do to avail themselves of the goodies lying on the corridor of his father's house.

He declared that it would require sacrifice to be slammed down on the corridor with coconut to serve the head. Thereafter all the instruments of prosperity, money, marriage and childbirth would come within the reach of the person making the sacrifice.

When it appears at divination, the person will be advised that his prosperity lies in his father's house in the land of his birth. He should not travel outside his home-base in quest of prosperity, because the consequences would be regrettable. He should stay home.

Chapter **6**

OWANRIN-OKONRON

```
II  II
II  II
II  I
I   I
```

He made Divination for The Guinea Fowl To Outlive Her Enemies:

Owanrin kpo kokan, Awo aworo, odifa fun aworo ni jo ti aawon
ota re fe kpaa je. Ebo ni oru-o.

He made divination for the guinea-fowl when her enemies were plotting to kill her for food. She was told to make sacrifice with a he-goat to Èsù and to serve her head with white and red kola nuts. She made the sacrifice after which Orunmila prepared medicine with tree branch and dried leaves, added the iyerosun of the odù and tied them up for the guinea-fowl to be keeping at the place where she slept

The hunter and the boa also went to Owanrin-Okonron for divination and they were told to serve; Èsù with a he-goat, and their heads with guinea-fowl. Without serving Èsù with he-goat, both the hunter and the boa went in search of the guinea-fowl in the forest. The boa saw the guinea-fowl and her children on top of a tree and was waiting for them to come down to launch an attack.

At the same time, after a long search, the hunter heard the cry of the guinea-fowl and her children in the forest. As soon as the hunter sighted the tree on which the guinea-fowls were resting, he moved stealthily to the foot of the tree. It was at that stage that Ighoroko, the herald-friend of Èsù, told him that it was the guinea-fowl alone that made sacrifice and that both the hunter and the boa failed to make sacrifice. When the hunter took aim with his gun to shoot the guinea-fowls, Èsù immediately startled them by shaking the branch of the tree on which they were resting. Instantaneously, the guinea-fowl and her children flew away.

Unknown to the hunter, Èsù had used dried leaves to conceal the boa on the ground. He could not see that he was standing on the snake. After the guinea-fowls flew away, the hunter stepped backwards treading on the tail of the boa, who instantaneously hit him with his venomous arrow. As soon as the hunter felt the bite of the boa, he cut a pointed stick to pierce down on the head of the boa before using his cutlass to cut its head and tail. The hunter hurried home to apply medicine on the snakebite. Before he got home, the poison had overrun his circulatory system, and he began to vomit. He just managed to reach home before he died.

That was how sacrifice enabled the guinea-fowl to outlive the enemies who were gunning for her. When it appears at Ugbodu, the person should be told to prepare his Èsù immediately with a he-goat so that the new Ifa, with the cooperation of Èsù, would destroy the two powerful enemies who are after him.

The Divination Made for Him When He Was Leaving Heaven:

Eni konron, Olakonron, Eroni su se amikon.
Work today, work tomorrow, but no one works all the time
Merrily shall I sleep and cheerfully shall I wake.

Those were the Awos who made divination for this odu when he was coming to the world. He was told that if he made sacrifice, he would be able to weather the storm the enemies were going to ferment for him as a result of his success. He was told to make sacrifices to: his head with a guinea-fowl and coconut; his guardian angel with a castrated he-goat to feast the higher powers; Èsù with a he-goat; and Ogun with cock, dog and tortoise. He left for the world after making all the sacrifices.

On getting to the world he took to trading in addition to Ifa practice and he was always moving about. He succeeded both as a trader and as an Ifa priest, but his prosperity gave no comfort to his relations, who contrived all kinds of problems for him. His wives and children were often falling ill and he was spending a lot of money for taking care of them. He subsequently went for divination and he was advised to give a he-goat to Èsù and a rabbit to the elders of the night.

After enjoying his he-goat, Èsù brought pressure to bear on Ogun and the night to fight the enemies of Owanrin-Konron. His enemies began to die one after the other, and he was subsequently left to thrive in peace.

When it appears at Ugbodu, the person should be told that he would flourish in any business he does, but should make sacrifice to negate the evil plans of his own relations against him.

He Made Divination for The Oba-Ajigbomekon Akira When He Was Ill:

The Oba-ajigbomekon was seriously ill and all known Awos were invited to cure him without success. That was the point at which Owanrin-Okonron was invited to assist him. Owanrin-Okonron was not just an Ifa priest. He was also using the powers of Osanyin to achieve his objectives. He had one charm which was capable of obeying his command and of doing whatever he wanted it to do.

When he got to Oja-ajigbomekon, he made divination for the Oba and told him to make sacrifice and to have a bath with a medicine he was going to prepare for him. He was to make the sacrifice with a hen and a cock. The sacrifice was made after which he brought out his diabolical charm (sigidi in Yorùbá and amaze in Bini) anointed it with alligator pepper and a three-piece kola nuts. Thereafter Owanrin-Okonron commanded the charm to point at the direction of whatever was responsible for the Oba's illness. Straightaway, the charm moved to the bottom of the throne on which the Oba was sitting, and it began to dance under the chair. Owanrin-Okonron requested the Oba to get up from the chair. It was then they found all kinds of destructive charms under the chair. They were all removed and dumped in a pit latrine. Thereafter, he prepared medicine for the Oba to bath in. After having the bath, the Oba was able to sleep soundly for the first time in several months.

Within the next three days, the Oba had become completely well. That achievement launched Owanrin-Okonron into fame and he subsequently became the diviner and physician of all the kings and aristocracy of the known world.

When this Ifa appears at Ugbodu, the person will be an effective traditional doctor but should be advised not to boast. He should make regular offerings to the night because they will assist him in his work. He should prepare Osanyin or Osun for his Ifa, and serve it with a cock and a tortoise. He will succeed in whatever he does on earth.

At divination, the person should serve the Osanyin or Osun of his family or the one he has at home. He should forbid roasted corn and beware of over-generosity.

He Made Divination for The Cockroach, Lizard and The Rat:

Owanrin Mukuku si odo, was the Awo who made divination for the Cockroach, Lizard and Rat, advising them to make sacrifice in order to have a brighter life. They did not make the sacrifice. On the other hand, Igbankan gboroo made divination for the fish advising him to make sacrifice to survive an attack from his enemies. He made the sacrifice with okra, hand fish and sheer butter (ori-oyo).

Meanwhile, the Lizard, Cockroach and Rat, requested the Cat to catch fish for them in the river. On account of the sacrifice which the fish made, his body became too slippery for the cat to handle. The cat made several abortive efforts until he caught a cold. By the time he got home, Èsù told him to feast on those who sent him on a wild goose chase. It was from then on that the cat began to feed on lizard, rat and cockroach.

When it appears at divination, the person will be told that some people are contriving evil plans against him. He will be advised to make sacrifice to neutralize their machinations. He should also be warned never to plan evil against others, lest he would lose his life in the process.

This Odu's Sacrifice for Prosperity:

Odoro mi owo kiribi, was the Awo who made divination for the fish, the dog and the crab. They were told to make sacrifice with a pigeon and a rat, to enable them to have free food to eat. They made the sacrifice which is why they do not struggle too much for their daily bread.

When it appears at divination the person will be advised to make sacrifice so that he does not toil too hard for his daily bread.

Divination For any Group To Have a Leader:

Ifa ni were ko were jo. Emina ni were ko were jo.
Moni kini je be. Ifa ni omo eranko. Oni won ko ra
won jo. Won ko ni olori. Oni were ko were jo ni.

Orunmila said that lunatics congregate with lunatics.
He explained that it was a figure of speech meaning.

That the animals and birds of the forest congregate without appointing a king among them, and that be it men, animals, birds who congregate without appointing a leader, are a crazy lot. To appoint a leader, he recommended sacrifice with rat, fish, akara, eko and he-goat, and thereafter choose a king or leader among them, just as Oduro is put on the throne to head all ikin.

When it appears at divination for a group of people, they will be told that all of them are equals.

When this odu appears at divination, the person will be advised to make prescribed sacrifices to avert the danger of the sudden death of his wife. If it appears for a woman, she will be warned not to take undue advantage of her husband's love to demand favors fraught with fatal consequences for herself and her husband.

Chapter 7

OWANRIN-IROSUN
OWANRIN-LOGBON
OWANRIN-EWI

```
I  II
I  II
II  I
II  I
```

The Divination Made for Him Before Leaving Heaven:

Erin Lere, mi Erin Lere.

Smiling brings favor, was the name of the Awo who made divination for him before leaving heaven. He was advised to make sacrifice to avert the risk of becoming temperamental on earth.

He was warned that impatience and irritability would make prosperity to elude him. He was told not to rely too heavily on the advice of friends. He was therefore advised to serve Èsù on the bush path with 2 pigeons, 2 gourds of palm wine, 16 kola nuts, rat, fish and a dog. After the sacrifice, he was to have a bath on the spot, while leaving all the sacrificial materials there.   Next, he was to; feast his guardian angel with a piece of white cloth, parrot's feather, castrated he-goat, gourd of palm wine, 201 cowries and eagle's feather; serve Ogun with a he-goat, cock, tortoise, dog, snail and rolled fish and to persuade Ògún to follow him to the world; and to serve Èsù-Obadara with a he-goat. After making the sacrifices, Ogun gave him a sledge hammer and a scissors, while agreeing to follow him to the world, provided he did not neglect him. He then left for the world.

On getting to earth, he built his house near the source of river Osa, (God's own river), which is the route traditionally taken by God when He comes to earth. As soon as he built the house, he began to practice Ifism. One day, he was away from home when God passed by his house, but the Almighty Father left a piece of white cloth, a white chalk, an eagle's feather and a parrot's feather, at the entrance to his house. When he returned home to meet the strange gifts, he began to wonder who might have left them there. He sought advice from his colleagues, who told him that it was a presentiment designed to warm him. He subsequently threw them into the river.

Nine days later, God saw the materials he threw into the river and wondered what kind of man could afford to reject His own divine gifts. God however deposited the same materials at the entrance of his house after adding a red scimitar and a pair of Ogun's scissors. When he returned home to find the same materials and the new ones, he went again to his friends, who scared him by telling him that there was an evil force who did not want him to remain in the house. He subsequently abandoned his house and proceeded to live elsewhere.

Up to that time he had no wife and child. All his colleagues were prospering, but he continued to languish in abject penury. At a point, he began to behave as if he had suffered a mental derangement, and he actually became a laughing stock. That was the point at which the Awo who made divination for him in heaven was visiting the world. One night, his guardian angel ordered him to leave at once for Orita-Ijaloko. Without knowing why he was to go there, he proceeded aimlessly to the boundary of heaven and earth.

As soon as he got there he saw an Ifa priest who was divining for other people and he too went to meet him. The Awo made divination for him and asked him why; he abandoned the gifts that God sent to him, and neglected Ogun, the divinity that followed him to the world. He was advised to give a he-goat to Èsù as soon as he got back home. He returned home to serve Èsù with a he-goat. After enjoying the he-goat, Èsù went at once to remind Ogun of the elaborate sacrifices that Owanrin-Irosun made to him in heaven, because the man was suffering on earth.

Ogun quickly left for Owanrin-Irosun's house where he met him in a state of paranoia. Ogun greeted him by slapping him on the face, which immediately made him to become possessed.

Thereafter, Ogun gave him a gong and a sledge hammer. With those two instruments on either hand, he began to dance and to sing strange songs, eventually running out from his house. Since the people around him had become familiar with his erratic behavior, they took his dancing, singing and running as a severe manifestation of his delirium, and so they followed him.

He made straight for his old house which he previously abandoned and began to hit his head with the gong and hammer in his hands. Next, he began frantically to look for God's gifts and they were still there intact at the entrance to his house. He then knelt down, thanked God, his guardian angel, and the Ogun that woke him up from a long slumber. People soon realized that whatever he was predicting and proclaiming were not only intelligible but very revealing. The people danced and sang with him for the better part of that evening. He however remained possessed and before the following morning, his hair had all coiled into a rasta as if he had neither washed nor combed them since he was born (Dada in Yorùbá and Agbihiagha in Bini). He soon began to perform wonders and it was then that people realized that he was an Ogun priest.

The other divine priests got together and assisted him in building his Ogun shrine from where people began to consult him for divination. He operated simultaneously as an Orisa priest and as an Ogun priest and he was so successful that he subsequently got married and gave birth to several children.

When this odu appears at Ugbodu, the person should be told that he is an Ogun priest and should proceed without delay to perform the requisite initiation into the Ogun priesthood. He should be told not to discard any gift he receives in mysterious circumstances.

The Divination Made for Him When One of His Wives Misbehaved:

Over time, he became specialized in giving medicine for barren women to bear children. Meanwhile, another Awo seduced one of his wives. He did not bother unduly about it until the seducer began to boast that he did it with impunity because Owanrin-Irosun was incapable of doing anything. Meanwhile, Èsù asked him for a he-goat which he gave. Thereafter, Èsù went to the seducer's house and used the pad of a woman's menstrual discharge to neutralize all his protective powers. Before the following morning, the man ran mad and left the town never to be seen again. It was then that the woman went to beg her husband to accept her back. He told her to appease Ifa with a goat, Ogun with a cock, and Èsù with a he-goat. After making all the penitential sacrifices, she was given the traditional absolution, after which he accepted her back.

When this Ifa appears at Ugbodu, the person will be advised to beware of losing his life on account of a woman. He should be advised not to seduce another man's wife. To forestall that eventuality, he should serve; Èsù with a he-goat, a bat and a bird called Oge (Alevbe in Bini), and Ifa with a hen. He should be told to serve Ogun as conscientiously as he serves Ifa.

At divination, the person should serve Èsù with a he-goat to avoid having difficulties on account of a woman. He should be advised to move cautiously with a woman he is currently befriending.

He Made Divination for The People of Akoko:

Oshu waju omu ori kosun. Odafa fun won lode Akoko.

The man who moved forward with a load of salt on his head, was the Awo who made divination for the people of Ode-Akoko (Evboikhinmwin in Bini) when they were anxious to have children. He advised them to make sacrifice with a hen, 10 snails, a cock, kola nuts and palm oil. They made the sacrifice after which women began to have children again at Akoko.

That is the sacrifice which barren women will be required to make if this Ifa appears for her at divination. He also made a similar sacrifice for a barren woman called Onitide, before she started having children, and one of her children became very famous. At divination, the person should be advised to beware of making jest of an elderly person who could curse him with ASE because the curse would manifest.

Sacrifice against Fear and Anxiety:

When this odu appears at divination, the person should be told that he is afraid or anxious about something. Orunmila said that if a person is afraid, he should make sacrifice with rat, fish, pigeon and arrange to have his own Ifa. Orunmila will allay all his fears and worries and lead him to a life of eternal happiness and peace.

He Made Sacrifice for The People of Olukoro Against War:

The people of Olukoro were always living in fear and anxiety because they were frequently attacked by enemy forces and husbands and wives were consequently taken away into captivity. When they heard of Owanrin-Irosun, they sent for him to come and help them.

On getting to the town he made divination for them, advising them to make sacrifice to avert the risk of another devastating attack. They made the sacrifice with the meat of bush animals, a strong he-goat and a pot. After making the sacrifice, he used the pot to make a drum covered with the skin of the he-goat. He advised them that from time to time, they were to beat the drum and Èsù would drive away potential danger from the town.

They did what Orunmila told them. At the end of three years of unprecedented peace and tranquility, all the men and women trooped out and began to sing and dance to the beating of the drum as follows:

Ojojumo ni ominu ma nko ni bi-ogun-bi-ogun.
Ojojumo ni eru ma mba eniyan bi ote-bi-ote,
Enia ni o gbe ikoko de igbo-irunmole,
ti ikoko si nda eru ba eni.
Babalawo Olukoro difa fun olukoro,
Awon, won gbo riru ebo ti won ru,
Awon, won gbo eru atukesu, ti won tu.
Ko i pe, ko i jina, won wa bami,
ni laru segun ebo.

Meaning:

Everyday used to bring the fear and threat of war.
Every day we were all tormented by the fear of war.
Until someone came to our rescue with a sacrificial pot.
The Ifa priest of Olukoro made divination for the people of Olukoro.
They listened to the advice and made the prescribed sacrifice.
Sacrifices manifest for those who make them.
It is a long time since our problems have gone behind us.
And now we are wining and dining in relative peace and merriment.

When this odu appears at divination, the person will be advised to make sacrifice and if possible to take to the musical profession, where lies his prosperity.

He Made Divination for Osumare:

Owanrin gbaja irosun, o fi we ori, ondifa fun Osumare.

He made divination for Osumare to give birth to an only child. Osumare was told to make sacrifice with a strong he-goat and the mother's loin cloth. He refused to make the sacrifice.

Not long afterwards, the child was born but it only lived for twenty-four hours. When it appears at divination, the person will be told that there is a very beautiful lady in his family who is pregnant. The woman is expecting a fay child (imere or igbakhuan) and should make sacrifice so that the child might be forced to stay in the world and become very famous.

Chapter **8**

OWANRIN-OGUNDA
OWANRIN-OGUNRERE
OWANRIN-OLOGBON

```
 I   II
 I   II
 I    I
II    I
```

He Made Divination for The Farm and The Surrounding Bush:

Edo lifi kanrikan shewu.
Adifa fun eba oko, abufun arinrin oko.
Aniki awon mejeji rubo.

The stick used to support the stalk of a germinating yam plant (eghee in Bini) coils the yam's stem as a sponge garment to cover its body. That was the name of the Awo who made divination for the farm and for the bush surrounding it. They were both advised to make sacrifice in order to enjoy the fruits of their labor.

The farm saw no reason why he had to make any sacrifice since he was the husband of all the crops in his domain and they would give birth to children that would enlarge the size of his family without being taken anywhere else. The bush surrounding the farm however made sacrifice with a laying hen and its eggs, and a cock, but failed to give a he-goat to Èsù.

When the yams were subsequently harvested, the tubers were stacked away in the surrounding bush because of its coolness. The farm was considered too hot from exposure to the rays of the sun. The surrounding bush became the abode of the products of the farm, but only for a time. Since none of them gave he-goat to Èsù, all the crops of the farm including the yam tubers were eventually taken to the house for consumption or sale and the farm was left high and dry.

When it appears at divination, the person should be told to make sacrifice so that the fruits of his efforts may not be reaped to benefit someone else.

He Divined for The King of Termites:

Owanrin ola; Erin lo gbo ohun orun ola l'on sa.
Efan lo gbo ohun okpolo lo f'ohun aro. Ogbigbo lo nsa
gun ori uroko. Orahun tan Onibi ara aiye koba gbo
oni ero orun amo. Kosi ohun todun bi kaji kara ale.
Adafa fun Olu ikan to ji to ko ru ebo.

The elephant heard the sound of the gaiter and ran away in fright.
The buffalo heard the voice of the toad and retorted with his own harsh voice.
The theokam (ogbigo in Yorùbá and owonwon in Bini) escaped to the top of the Iroko tree
to say that if the earth did not hearken to his nagging, the heavens would listen.
Nothing is as exhilirating as waking up in the morning with a sound and healthy body
and mind.

These were the names of the Awos who made divination for the king of termites living in the anthill, but who woke up in the morning without making sacrifice. That is why he woke up to discover to his dismay that he had become a limbless cripple. It rolls on the ground and is carried about by the ants since he has no hands and feet.

When it appears at divination, the person should be told that he owes the debt of one sacrifice which he has not made. That is the cause of the illness he is concealing. The sacrifice which the king of termites did not make was to serve; Èsù with a he-goat, and his head with a pigeon and a cock.

That is the sacrifice the person should make if not already ill, that is, if it is Uree. But if he or she is already ill and it is Ayeo, the person should make the same sacrifices, adding the king of termites.

The Divination He Made Before Leaving Heaven:

Agbe d'ale, Aluko do owuro, were the Awos who made divination for this odu when he was coming to the world. He was told to make sacrifice in order to succeed in his work on earth. He was to make sacrifice with; he-goat to Èsù; a ram and unsplit kola nuts fruit to his guardian angel; dog, cock, tortoise, red cloth, and roasted yam to Ogun; and to serve Elenini, the Obstacle divinity with all eatable foodstuffs on the eve of his departure to the world. He made all the sacrifices but forgot to send all edible foodstuffs to Elenini (Idoboo in Bini) before travelling. His guardian angel however advised him to obtain the blessing (ASE) of God before leaving, which he could not do because the Obstacle divinity blotted the message out of his mind for failing to give him food.

On Getting To The World, He Became a Practicing Ifa Priest:

Almost immediately, the Obstacle divinity (Elenini or Idoboo) set out on his trail to disrupt his activities. Before getting married, he was hailed as an up-and-coming Ifa priest. Within a short time, his proficiency had given him recognition at the royal court and he was made one of the king's diviners.

One morning, the "erudite awo" as he was called in the palace, was invited by Olofin for divination. After completing his work at the palace, he met a very pretty woman with whom he fell in love at first sight and who lost no time in requiting his affection. The woman was sent to him by the Obstacle divinity, and she was head and shoulder stronger than Owanrin-Ogunda, because apart from having all the esoteric vigor of Elenini, she was herself the powerful queen of the cult of witchcraft (Iyami Osoronga in Yorùbá and Oghidian-ni-ya'son in Bini).

They got married almost immediately and she moved in to live with Orunmila. No sooner had she moved into his life, than his fortune began to wane. Without any justification whatsoever, his colleagues began to find faults with him. Even the Olofin began to reproach him because his predictions were no longer coming true.

He could not identify the cause of his problems, because the most difficult problem to identify is the one living, sleeping and waking up with one at home. His fortune had deteriorated so remarkably that he became a laughing stock.

When he eventually met a visiting Awo, he asked for divination, at which he was told to serve Èsù with a he-goat and his Ifa with a hen, ram and an unsplit kola nut. He performed the sacrifices without any delay. Thereafter the Awo prepared leaves to wash his Ifa, and to bath the evil hands of misfortune from his body. A number of Awos participated in the ceremony because it was as if he was rejuvenating his Ifa and himself, because he had erstwhile lost his instrument of authority (ASE).

After having the bath, it was time to split the kola nut fruit. All the Awos present were told to forecast the number of kola nuts in the fruit. Some said, 4, others 5,6,7,8 and so on. When he was told to make his own forecast, he said that there were three kola nuts in the fruit case. The officiating Ifa priest (Ojugbona) also predicted that the fruit had three kola nuts. When it was eventually split, it was found to contain three kola nuts which was an indication that his ASE was already coming back to him.

Soon after the sacrifice, his wife became ill and he spent all the money he had to cure her, but she did not become well. His own work was returning to normal and he was being acclaimed once more.

He Returns With Others To Heaven for Renewal of ASE:

When people saw the speed with which his ASE returned to him, clients began to flock to him for consultation on how to renew their own ASE. Ogun was the first to come for divination. After divination he advised Ogun to return to heaven to renew his ASE from God, but that before going, he should make sacrifice to: Èsù with a he-goat, Ifa with a hen, and his (Ogun's) guardian angel with a dog and a tortoise. Ogun only served Ifa but refused to serve Èsù and his own guardian angel. Thereafter, he left for heaven.

As soon as Ogun left, three other Awos, Agbe (Ukhiokhio in Bini), Aluko (Awe in Bini) and Odie (Okhue in Bini) also came to Orunmila for divination. It was his own odu (Owanrin-Ogunda) that came out of all three of them.   He also advised them to return to heaven to have their ASE renewed. He advised each of them to serve; Èsù with he-goat, Ifa with hen and Ogun with dog, cock, tortoise, roasted yam, palm oil and palm wine. All three of them threw up their hands in despair, complaining that they could not fund such elaborate sacrifices. All the same, they left for heaven to renew their instruments of authority (ASE).

After his clients had left, Orunmila also consulted Ifa and it was his own odu (Owanrin-Ogunda) that also appeared, which meant that he too had to perform the same sacrifice that he enjoined others to make, before going to heaven to renew his ASE.

In spite of the fact that he had just completed his own set of sacrifices, he proceeded nonetheless to serve:- Èsù with another he-goat; Ifa with a hen; and since Ogun had already left for heaven, Ifa told him to travel in his bag with a whole tuber of roasted yam, palm oil and palm wine, and to leave the dog, tortoise and cock at Ogun's shrine against his return from heaven.

In consonance with the divination, he travelled with all the materials. His departure coincided with the time of Ogun's return from heaven after obtaining a new ASE. He was already very hungry and tired, and so decided to sit down by the side of the road to rest. The first traveller to meet Ogun was Agbe. When Ogun asked him whether he did not make any divination before leaving home, Agbe replied that he indeed made divination with Orunmila and that the Ifa that appeared for him was Owanrin-Oguntan. The way he pronounced the name of the odu sounded as if he had sacriligiously referred to Ogun as a finished divinity. That made Ogun to become paranoid and he got up in a frenzy to behead Agbe with his sword, keeping his head in his bag, after drinking the blood.

Aluko was the next traveller to meet Ogun. When Ogun also asked him whether he made divination before leaving home, Aluko answered that he did indeed and that the Ifa which appeared for him was Owanrin-Eguntan. Since the pronunciation of the odu profaned Ogun's divine dignity, he again reacted deliriously by chopping off Aluko's head with his sword and pocketing his head after drinking the blood. It was exactly the same fate that the third traveller, Odide suffered in Ogun's hands, which meant that all the three people who refused to make sacrifice before leaving home had suffered the loss of their own lives.

When Ogun eventually met Orunmila, his eyes were already red as if he had been charged for combat. He however greeted Orunmila reverently as his Awo, before asking him whether he did not make any divination before leaving him. Orunmila confirmed that he did and that it was his own odu - which he called Owanrin-Ogunrere - that appeared for him and that he also made the required sacrifices. Since the way he pronounced the name of his Ifa was tantamount to a praise for Ogun, the eyes of the fire divinity simmered down. He was now seemingly happy. Ogun however asked Orunmila whether he was not told to serve Ogun. Orunmila confirmed that he was advised to serve Ogun and that was the point at which he brought out the roasted yam and palm oil in his bag. After Ogun had eaten the yam with the palm oil, Orunmila gave him the gourd of palm wine to top it up. He then told Ogun that he had left the other materials at his (Ogun's) shrine at home since he was away.

That was why and how Ogun gave this odu the nickname of "Owanrin-Ologbon", that is, the wise and intelligent Ifa priest.

At that stage Èsù intervened by stimulating Ogun to use his newly acquired ASE to pray for Orunmila to get to heaven safely and to acquire his own ASE on the same day without any delay. Since whatever Ogun said with his ASE was bound to happen, Orunmila thanked him for the good wishes. Ogun also gave Orunmila the heads of Agbe, Aluko and Odide, which made him to appreciate the fact that he had just survived a brush with death.

Orunmila subsequently went to heaven where he met several divinities and persons who had been waiting for months. As soon as God sighted Orunmila, he invited him at once and gave him a renewed ASE in consonance with Ogun's wishes for him. He swallowed the ASE and left for home immediately.

On getting home, he went to his Ifa shrine to curse whoever had been responsible for all the problems he had been encountering. His obscurantist wife died in her sleep before the following morning. Thereafter, Olofin invited him for a rapprochement and gave him the title of generalissimo (olori-egbe) of all the Awos in his kingdom. He married other wives and had many children subsequently. That is why it is not advisable to pronounce Ogunda as Oguntan or Eguntan, because Ogun will take umbrage to it.

When this Ifa appears at Ugbodu, the person should be advised to have his own Ogun prepared for him without any delay. He should also serve Ifa and Èsù so that he would excel in his work. He should also pay the debt of sacrifice his Ifa owes to the Obstacle divinity by collecting all eatable foodstuffs and adding a dog for sacrifice at a road junction for Elenini of Idoboo. If he is already married, he should ask his wife to deposit the sacrifice at the road junction. He should look carefully and deeply before marrying any woman. He should add the skulls or Agbe, Aluko and Odide to a he-goat for Èsù.

He Made Divination for a Woman Called Gbeyide When She Was Desperately Fretting To Have a Child:

She had already reached the climatic period of her life. Nonetheless when Orunmila made divination for her, Ifa revealed that in spite of the fact that she had attained the stage of menopause, she had a better than even chance of having children if she could make sacrifice. She was required to make sacrifice with the dress she was wearing (buba and iro) at the time of divination, in addition to a black goat and a U-bolt (aban). She was also required to serve her late father with a cock. Orunmila assured her that she could still have two male and one female children. She made the sacrifice without any delay.

On her way home after making the sacrifice she surprisingly started her menstruation. When she got home she reported the situation to her husband, who was surprised because her menopause began a couple of years ago. She subsequently became pregnant at the end of that month, and in the fullness of time, gave birth to a male child. The next child was also a boy while the last one was a girl.

When the eldest son was growing up, he began to demonstrate a flair for inventiveness. The second son also exhibited similar tendencies. Right from childhood, the girl also displayed signs of being a potential trader.

When she eventually went to Orunmila to make divination on the significance of the wonderful propensities of her children, Ifa revealed that; the senior son was an Ogun priest, the second son was a Sàngó priest, while the girl was from the kindred of the divinity of wealth (Iya-Alaje in Yorùbá and Igbaagnon in Bini).

Orunmila advised Gbeyide on the kind of food to be giving to each of her children. They grew up to become famous and prosperous.

When this Ifa appears at Ugbodu, the person will be told that there are three divinities that Ifa brought with him to the world. He should; prepare Ogun for his Ifa, provide his shrine with a thunder stone, as well as preparing Olokun for the Ifa.

He should serve Èsù with a he-goat and remove the dresses he or she was wearing on that occasion and leave them on the Èsù shrine, because they are his/her poverty or hard-luck garments. He should also serve Ifa with 4 pigeons which are to reared.

At divination, the person should have his bath while wearing discardable dresses, which have to be removed and left on Èsù shrine. The ceremony is done with a he-goat which after killing, the person will not eat out of the meat. He should also serve Ogun with a cock.

Orunmila's Sacrifice for Intelligence:

Orunmila advised his children to develop the qualities of quick-wittedness and awareness, because it is intelligence that enables the children of rats, fish, birds, animals and mankind to endure and survive the stresses and tensions of existence. When his children asked him the sacrifice to be made to acquire the aptitudes of awareness and intelligence, he told them to obtain the brain of a mother-cow and put it inside the Ifa plate overnight. The following day, it should be removed from the Ifa plate, and cooked with palm oil and salt, without adding pepper. After being cooked, it should be brought before the Ifa priest to add the divination powder (iyerosun) of the relevant odu and to recite the appropriate incantation after which the person will eat it.

This preparation is made when this Ifa appears at Ugbodu and also at divination for someone involved in doing brain work.

Divination for Correcting The Paradox of Existence:

Orunmila declared that there was something wrong when a square peg was put in a round hole. His children asked him what went wrong and he disclosed that no matter could be truly resolved until it is settled right.

He went on to explain that it was because:

(a) When the kingship of rats went to the wrong rat (asin), he became a misfit and he began to kill other rats. A reign of peace and comradeship took over when Asin was deposed and Torofini was appointed the king of rats;

(b) When the crab was made the king of fishes, there was a reign of terror, until the crayfish was appointed in his place and he ushered in the principle of live and let live;

(c) The snake kindred saw hell-fire when they appointed the python as their king because he began to swallow up the smaller snakes. They only became happy when the kingship went to the persevering boa;

(d) The birds suffered an epoch of cannibalism when the hawk was their king. They only had peace of mind when the proud peacock (okin) took over the throne.

Orunmila recalled that the sacrifice to be made for things to go right required; 10 rats (eku-toro mewa) and the leaves of ewe-eleto.

When it appears at divination, the person will be told that he has been outmaneuvered from his rightful position. He should make sacrifice so that the error could be corrected.

Chapter **9**

OWANRIN-OSA
OWANRIN-PISIN
OWANRIN-GA-ASA

```
II  II
I   II
I   I
I   I
```

He Made Divination for The Shaving Knife and The Cloth Used for Insulating Its Handle:

ka fi ota lo'ogun .Ka fi ogun l'ota.
Adifa fun Abe, abufun ododi eyin re.
Aniki awon mejeji ru ebo.
Abe ni kon lo ru ebo na.

The stone grinds medicine as the medicine grinds the stone. That was the name of the Awo who made divination for the shaving knife and the cloth used for covering its handle. They were both advised to make sacrifice with a hen. It was the knife alone that made the sacrifice. After a long span of cooperation and comradeship, the knife began to eat up the cloth.

When it appears at divination, the person will be advised to beware of a close associate who will gradually deprive him of his belongings trickishly. If it appears for a man or woman proposing to get married, he or she should be told to make sacrifice because the spouse would contrive devious stratagem to consume up his or her belongings.

He Made Divination for Orisa-Nla:

Owanrin wo ile Osa, wo ile Orisa.
Ubule aba wo lololo.
Won difa fun Orisa-Nla Oshereigbo ni gba
ti ara kon kon she.

They made divination for Orisa-Nla when he was indisposed. He was told to make sacrifice with 4 snails, a hen, a cock, a pigeon and white cloth. He made the sacrifice and he became well.

When it appears at divination for an invalid, he or she will be told that he/she has one divinity or Osanyin (Osun) at a corner in his/her shrine with white cloth on it. He should be told that its shrine is dirty and that he has not served it for a long time. That is what is responsible for his indisposition. He should serve it with four snails and paint the shrine with white emulsion and spread a piece of white cloth on it.

The Divination Made for Him in Heaven:

Mi gara lere, migara gara lere ni agbo ohun Ogun.

Those were the Awos who made divination for this odu when he was leaving heaven for the world. He was told to make sacrifice for long life and prosperity on earth. He was told to serve; his guardian angel with a ram and a crocodile, so that his enemies would give him a chance to achieve his objectives; Ogun with dog, cock and tortoise; Sàngó with ram and cock; and Èsù with 2 he-goats. He was warned to expect problems from Ogun and Sàngó.

Since he had no means of funding the elaborate sacrifices, he did as much as he could by giving; a ram and crocodile to his guardian angel, one he-goat to Èsù, a cock to Sàngó and tortoise to Ogun. Thereafter, he left for the world.

On getting to the world, he was depressed to see that his colleagues who came before him had not recorded any remarkable achievements. Since it was too late to retreat, he decided to weather the storm of survival on earth. The going was not easy for him, which frustrated him to the point of schizophrenia. That was his condition when there was an announcement by Sàngó that God was going to address the divinities on the evil inclinations of the world.

When the meeting was convened, all the divine priest and priestesses were invited to attend. As an Ifa priest, he too had to attend. As soon as all the invitees were assembled, God sat above on a suspended throne and began a tirade of admonitions for allowing Èsù to thrive so effectively on earth, that goodness had become a feeble and pale exception, while evil had become the general rule. God queried that He sent the divinities to the world to test whether Èsù could actually overwhelm them as he boasted at the beginning of time. That was when God warned that since the divinities and their human servants had become willing lackeys of Èsù, the divinity of evil, He was going to withdraw Truth to return to heaven and leave the earth to sink or swim with Falsehood and Èsù.

After God's invective diatribe, there was total silence. It was the inconsequential Owanrin-ga-Asa who eventually had the audacity to break the silence. He said that the Almighty Father was apportioning blame in the wrong direction, because it was within his power to make the world the paragon of excellence that He wanted it to be. He likened the world to a house built by its owner to accommodate his family comfortably. If the house begins to leak, and create inconvenience for its occupants, is it the rain and the occupants that are to blame or the owner who built a defective roof in the first place. Owanrin-ga-Asa emphasized that God was the creator of the imperfect world. As he was being hushed down by the elders, he began to shout at the top of his voice, that the failure of the divinities, mankind and the earth was not only a direct reflection of the fallacy of the maxims of God's own omniscience, omnipresence and infallibility, but an indication that Èsù had won the contest between good and evil.

Since no one was ever known to have spoken so intrepidly to God before that day, the poor fellow was about to be lynched by the others when God ordered them to leave him alone. The elders were so positive that his outburst was a confirmation that he had gone raven mad. At that stage God told the divinities to cure the man of his lunacy if they believed he was mad and gave them seven days to make him regain his sanity. After giving the assignment, God adjourned the meeting to be reconvened by Sàngó on the eight day.

It was Ogun that took the man home to look after him, but he was behaving so normally that the divinities decided to find out through divination what was actually wrong with him. The divinities made the necessary sacrifices for him but they were concerned that the man was quite sane.

On the eight day, Sàngó shouted to convene the meeting. As soon as all were assembled, God asked for the man who interrupted Him at the last meeting. Ogun brought him out to confirm that he was quite sane. In His own judgement, God concluded that everything he said was indisputable, and that the condition of the earth was a depressing proof of the victory of Èsù. That was where God warned that He was going to withdraw truth from earth before he was totally depraved by Èsù. That is why good people do not live long on earth. Owanrin-Osa was thus appointed to be holding meetings with all the divinities because it was he alone that had the courage to speak his mind. God ordained that no meeting of the divinities should hold unless Owanrin-ga-Asa was present. That incident marked the beginning of his prosperity.

When this Ifa appears at Ugbodu, the person should be told that he is very outspoken, and that he should always stick to the truth. He is likely to have mental derangement, but it will mark the arrival of prosperity into his life.

He Made Divination for Prince Borida:

Ibi to ori baa to maasun, ki ese mejeji si mi lo.
Odifa fun Borida omo oba l'ode otun.

Wherever the head will sleep is where the two legs carry it to. That was the name of the Awo who made divination for Borida, a prince who lived away from his home town. He was told to serve Èsù with a he-goat, 3 nails and a mini coffin. He made the sacrifice. He was subsequently taken away as a captive at the outbreak of war and sold into slavery. He was bought as a slave to the court of the Alara of Ilara. When Alara saw him, he found him so eloquent and endowed with such impressive physique, that he appointed him to be serving his (Alara's) head with two kola nuts every morning.

In carrying out the assignment, he prefaced it with his own aberration. He often used the kola nuts to serve his own feet to carry him wherever his head was destined to go, before using them to serve king Alara's head. After doing so for a while, a palace page who had been watching him, reported his impious action to the king. The Alara was so annoyed that he wanted to execute him, but he was reminded that a king is forbidden to kill anyone who serves his head. The Alara then ordered that Borida should be resold into slavery.

He was subsequently sold to the Ajero of Ijero who once more appointed him to be serving his head every morning. At Ajero, he continued his routine of serving his own feet and head with kola nuts before using them to serve the Ajero's head. That earned him the wrath of the Ajero who ordered him to sold into slavery. He was eventually sold into slavery to the Orangun of Illa and finally to the Oba of Benin.

The Oba of Benin did not sell him into slavery after discovering that he was often using kola nuts to serve his own feet and head before using them to serve his (Oba's) head. The Oba gave orders for a coffin to be prepared by the brass-smiths of Igun-eronmwon. He also asked the royal iron-smiths to prepare three giant nails. After putting white and oiled-crushed yams into the coffin, Borida was made to lie inside it. The coffin was covered up with its lid and the three giant nails were used to nail down the positions of his head, chest, and waist. On account of the sacrifice he had previously made to Èsù, the latter prevented the nails from impacting on his body.   Thereafter, the Oba gave orders that the coffin should be jettisoned into the river as a sacrifice to Olokun. The current of the river eventually carried the coffin into the sea.

The Oba of Otun had long died and when the kingmakers made divination on the appoint-ment of a new king, they were told that the next king was not going to come from the town of Otun but from the sea. They were told to be watching out for the direction of the waves of the sea every morning.

As the current was carrying him away, he was feeding on the crushed yam inside it, until the coffin was carried to the embarkment, of Otun. When it got there, the coffin began to turn round in a circular vortex. Èsù stopped it from going beyond that point.

When the sea-watchers saw a coffin engulfed in a whirlpool, they ran home to invite the elders, who gave instructions for divers to retrieve it. When they opened the coffin, they found a healthy handsome male adult inside it. He was brought out and given water to drink and food to eat. One of the elders who came with a walking stick to see the coffin was one of the advisers of the late Oba of Otun. When the old man looked squarely at the face of the strange man from the sea, he recognized him as the Oba's son who was long ago taken away as a war captive and presumed dead. The old man called him by his name Borida, and he answered. The old man then explained that the man was the crown prince they had long been looking for. He was immediately crowned as the Oba of Otun, in succession to his father.

Three months after his coronation, he invited all the Obas whose heads he earlier served. After feasting them elaborately, he asked whether they recognized him, but none of them could place him. He subsequently identified himself as Borida, the slave who was sold into slavery from the palace of Alara through Ijero and Orangun-Illa to Oba Ado-Ajuwaleke, for serving his own feet and head before serving their own. He then explained how his feet finally carried his head back to the land of his birth to be crowned as Oba of Otun. None of the Obas knew that he was a prince. They all rejoiced with him amidst drumming, dancing and merriment, he sang in praise of Owanrin-ga-Asa, who made divination and sacrifice for him.

When it appears at Ugbodu, the person should be told to be serving his head from time to time because he came from heaven with a crown, which he would surely wear later in life, after a long suffering, provided he makes sacrifice. At divination, the person should be told to serve Èsù with a he-goat because of a position of authority which he would attain through thick and thin.

He Made Divination for The Deaf and Dumb Woman:

He made divination for a deaf and dumb woman called Akitikori, who was so helpless that she contemplated committing suicide. She was subsequently advised to go to Orunmila for divina-tion, who advised her to make sacrifice to her guardian angel with a hen and to serve Èsù with a small he-goat, which was to be slaughtered and left on the shrine. Orunmila assured her that she would have a settled life after making the sacrifices. She subsequently made the sacrifices.

The woman, in spite of her physical handicaps, was a herbalist and physician. One day, a man called Emi came to her for medicine to cure his sight problem. She went to the forest to pick the appropriate leaves which she prepared for the man to be washing his eyes. The man told her he had been moving from one house to another because his enemies wanted him to become totally blind. He appealed to the woman to let him live with her and she readily agreed. They soon fell in love with each other and within a short time the woman became pregnant, and gave birth to a male child. The couple became very happy.

When this Ifa appears at Ugbodu, the person will be asked whether he has a deaf and dumb person in his family. If not, he should make sacrifice to prevent him from giving birth to a deaf or dumb child, and to avoid the risk of eye trouble. He should give a small he-goat to Èsù which would be split on the shrine, adding a kola nut that has no pieces (alakriboto in Yorùbá and egbian in Bini).

At divination, the person should serve Èsù with a he-goat and the small animal called emi in Yorùbá and erin in Bini, adding a red parrot's feather.

Orunmila's Special Sacrifice for Prosperity:

Orunmila ni otekeleje agbon. It is one's head that leads one to prosperity. It was a good head that crowned the king of Ilara; it was his good head that led Orangun to become king of Illa-Orangun. It was a good head that led Orungun to become the king of Ila-Orangun. It was a good head that led the Oba of Otumoba to become the king of Otumoba. It was a good head that made Ajaponda the king of Akure. It was a good head that became the Oba of Benin, Omo areyo-okun-meji-tayo-gbere-gbere. The same is true of the Alaafin of Oyo and the Ooni of Ife.

When he was asked for the sacrifice to be made in order to choose a good head, he said that whoever this odu appears for at divination must arrange without delay to have his own Ifa. He recommended sacrifice to Ifa with pounded yam put inside a calabash plate (ugba) with soup, 2 kola nuts, all stacked in a basket. After having his Ifa and making the sacrifice, the person will surely attain a position of authority in life.

When it appears at divination, the person should be advised to serve his head and make sacrifice with rabbit and snail. He should have his own Ifa if the divinee is a man or ask the husband to have Ifa if she is a woman. That is the only way of achieving the prosperity that is in store for them.

Chapter 10

OWANRIN-ETURA
OWANRIN-ELEJIGBO

```
 I    II
II    II
 I    I
 I    I
```

Made Divination for The Tortoise When He Was Having Land Dispute With The Elephant:

Ebiti kpale mole.
Odifa fun Oloba-aghun ni jo to'nlo
ba erin du ale baba re.

He made divination for the tortoise when he was contesting the ownership of his father's land with the elephant. The elephant was the first to go for divination, but he refused to make the prescribed sacrifice for him because he felt that the tortoise would have no ground to stand with him in a contest.

On the other hand the tortoise was told to make sacrifice with a he-goat and beans. After the sacrifice, the Ifa priest gave him the beans to plant all over the land. Meanwhile the elephant went to the land and walked all over it in a way that his footprints became clearly visible all over that place. The Awos advised the tortoise not to bring issues to a head until the beans germinated and spread. The tortoise therefore laid low until he was sure that the beans grew and spread throughout the length and breadth of the land in dispute.

Thereafter, the tortoise brought the matter to the king and elders for adjudication. The tortoise threatened to wage a war on the elephant if they did not deliberate on the matter early enough. They advised him not to fight and to give them a chance to decide the case. Meanwhile, the elephant and the tortoise were subpoenaed to appear before the court of the king-in-council.

When the elephant was told to assert his title to the ownership of the land, he said that his footprints and those of his father could be seen all over the land and that he had recently weeded the shrubby on it. When the tortoise was told to establish his claim on the land, he started by putting a question to the court. Whether that piece of land was the only expanse of land on which the elephant had ever treaded, and whether there were no other pieces of land not belonging to his father on which their footprints could be seen? After apparently succeeding in casting aspersion on the veracity of the elephant's claim, he proceeded to say that his father used to farm on the land, and that the principal crop he planted was beans. He said that he was sure that traces of the remnants of beans could still be found on the land at that very moment.

At that point, the elders sent people to go and verify the landmarks established by the contestants. Before the investigators got to the land, shrubs had grown to cover the footprints of the elephant. They could only see two foot marks of the elephant and there was nothing to substantiate the point made by the elephant that he had recently brushed the shrubs.

On the other hand, they discovered that beans had grown all over the land, a clear proof that the land had previously been used for planting beans. When the verifiers reported their findings to the Oba-in-council, they had no hesitation in arriving at a consensus that the land belonged to the tortoise's father. The right of ownership was thereby given to the tortoise.

When this odu appears at divination, the person should be asked whether he or she has a pending land dispute with anyone. If he or she so confirms, then sacrifice would have to be made to avoid losing the land to his rival, who might establish indelible landmarks on it.

He Made Divination for The Palm Tree and The Umbrella Tree:

Ibara ni ile oko. Koro yara ni ile ada. Adifa fun okpe,
abufun odan tori obinrin shango.

The overhead counter of the house is the abode of the hoe. The corner of the room is the resting place of the cutlass. These were the names of the Ifa priests who made divination for the Palm tree and Umbrella tree (Odan in Yorùbá and Obadan in Bini) when they were flirting with Shango's wife. They were advised to make sacrifice to forestall the wrath of Shango. None of them made the sacrifice.

When Shango eventually became aware of their flirtatious move towards his wife, he descended to tear the two of them to death with his axe. That is why the two trees are prone to attacks by thunder.

At divination, the person should be warned to ignore any woman who professes love to him during that period, in order to avert the risk of sudden death or a long-lasting sickness. If he is already having a relationship with a woman, he should make sacrifice to prevent any adverse consequences. If it appears for a marriage proposal, the man should be told to give up the woman because she would eventually bring about his destruction or death.

The Divination Made for Him Before Leaving Heaven:

Bebe tutu, Oni tutu bebe, made divination for this odu when he was leaving heaven. He was a do-gooder conciliator, and peacemaker, who was determined to make the world more livable for its inhabitants. News had been reaching heaven that Èsù had instigated the ferocious divinities to heat up the entire earth. Owanrin-Etura was determined to go and cool down the earth. At divination, he was advised to make sacrifice to: the wind divinity with a fan made of feathers (abebe in Yorùbá and ezuzu in Bini) and two pigeons; his guardian angel with honey, salt, snails and a goat; and Èsù with a he-goat, adding all edible foodstuffs. After making the sacrifices, his guardian angel directed him to obtain the blessing of God before leaving for earth. He went before the divine altar of God, and he received the blessing.

On getting to the world, he became a practicing Ifa priest. He did his utmost to make life easy on earth, but the place remained hot in spite of his efforts. Seeing that his effort was an inconsequential drop in the ocean of iniquities, he decided to return to heaven for further investigations. He met Èsù as soon as he reached heaven, who told him that the turbulence on earth was a function of the sanguinary tendencies of the vindictive divinities created by God. Èsù however, demanded and obtained a he-goat from Owanrin-Etura.

After eating his he-goat, Èsù went to the wind divinity to ask why he allowed so much heat to overwhelm the world. He replied that it was he (Èsù) who was fanning the embers of turmoil on earth. Èsù retorted that he had forgotten Owanrin-Etura who made sacrifice to him before leaving heaven to be able to cool the earth. While Èsù was challenging the wind divinity, Owanrin-Etura went to God to tell the Almighty Father about his failure to cool down the earth. That was when God invited the wind divinity to proceed without delay to cool down the earth. The wind divinity is one of the closest servants of God who He uses for special errands. The wind divinity reminded God that his place was by His side and in heaven. God however told him to be paying occasional visits to the earth to be cooling it down whenever it has overreached itself with heat. The wind divinity travelled to earth with the fan, his son, who he left on earth to operate when he is in heaven. Meanwhile, God cleared Owanrin-Etura to return to earth to await the arrival of the wind divinity.

When the wind finally reached the earth, he used the fan to blow away all the agents of iniquity and mischief, forcing most of them to return to heaven. Thereafter cool air gradually returned to earth. When the wind got to Orunmila's house, he told him that he had blown away all those responsible for heating up the earth and that thenceforth, he was going to have a better atmosphere in which to carry out his benevolent work. Before returning to heaven, he advised Orunmila that if anyone tried to heat up the world in his absence, he should use the fan, by using kola nuts to sprinkle water on them by saying;

OYI-RE, OYIRE, OYIRE, Oyi afe rio lara, Oyi afe mi lara.

That is the ritual that Ifa priests do to this day when they are serving Orunmila. The wind then gave the fan to Orunmila and returned to heaven. That is why no Ifa shrine can be complete without a fan. Thereafter Orunmila became very effective in the performance of his work.

When this Ifa appears at Ugbodu, the person will be told that his prosperity will come from virtuousness and uprightness. He should immediately provide a fan for his new Ifa, and serve it with 16 snails, honey and salt.

When it appears at divination, the person will be advised to have his own Ifa in order to make progress in his work. He has many detractors who are making life difficult for him. Orunmila will help him to scale all the hurdles on his path.

The Sacrifice He Made for Prosperity on Earth:

Orunmila pronounced deprivation, and his children confirmed that there was deprivation all over the earth. Orunmila observed that lack of children, money and the good things of life summed up to hardship, and hence required sacrifice. When he was asked for the sacrifice to be made, he enumerated the following; pigeons for riches, cock for marriage, a rabbit and a bat for having children, 16 snails to have peace of mind, a ram for elevation, he-goat to Èsù to coordinate all desires and a sheep for living to a ripe old age. When the sacrifice was being made, Orunmila sang the following song:

Ogbo eyele lu o re ode.
Temi taya ni yio ma sun.
Temi taya ni yio ma ji.
Eyele lo o re ode.
Temi tomo yio ma sun.
Temi tomo yio ma ji.
Eyele ni lu o re okun,
Temi tire ni yio ma sun.
Temi tire ni yio ma ji.
Ile kun ke-ke-ke ni ewure ma nke.
Igbin de omo alakoro pero simi ni'le.
Pero simi ni ona.
Temi tire ni yio ma sun.
Temi tire ni yio ma ji.
Ile kun ke-ke-ke ni ewure ma nke.
Igbin de omo alakoro pero simi ni'le.
Pero simi ni ona.
Temi tire ni yio ma sun.
Temi tire ni yio ma ji.
Ile kun ke-ke-ke ni ewure ma nke.
Igbin de omo alakoro pero simi ni'le
Pero simi ni ona.
Kini a fi eni se?
Ero gbodo, gbodo, gbodo, ero.
A o dagba, a o ni tete ku, a la loro aguntan.
Seni ori a ma fun g
Temi pe, temi pe ni ese aguntan ma ndun ni ori apata.
Agunde, a bori borogi.
Kaka ki'mi ku, ma fi ori e di'le
Ewe di'le di'le temi, di ona iku fun mi,
Ma di ona ere.

Meaning:

The aged pigeon flapped its wings and flew into
the distance.
My wife and I will always sleep and wake together.
The pigeon flapped its wings and flew away.
My children and I will always sleep and wake together.
The pigeon flew to the beach.
I shall always sleep and wake with good fortune.
The house is full, is the traditional cry of the goat.

The snail will bring its coolness to my house and my life.
What do we ask Ifa to do for us?
To bring us peace and prosperity and to help us to live,
To a ripe old age, and not to die prematurely.
Long life, is the sound made by the sheep's footsteps.
Ifa will prepare leaves to bury death for me, and
Open for me the path of eternal prosperity.

When this odu appears at divination, the person will be told that he is unduly worried about the future, because his life is not stable. He should make sacrifice in order to have a settled life of peace, rest of mind, and prosperity.

He Made Divination for Eighty-Four Birds:

Owanrin be yege yege yege, made divination for 84 birds to avert the problem of sleeplessness and strife. They were told to make sacrifice with fried corn and fried beans. All of them made the sacrifice with the exception of the duck.

When the birds got to the world, the duck developed trouble with the legs and was no longer able to work like other birds. When Èsù was told that the duck failed to make sacrifice, he decided to be tickling her from falling asleep. Any time she wanted to fall asleep, Èsù would blink his eyes to her. That is why ducks and drakes suffer from malignant insomnia.

When this odu appears at divination, the person should be advised to make sacrifice without delay to avert the risk of illness that could affect his legs and give rise to insomnia.

He Made Divination for The Akara Seller:

He made divination for an akara seller called Aje mgbele. Sankpana was the agent selling the akara for her, but the divinity of epidemic was in the habit of distributing the akara freely to people without collecting money for them. The woman was too scared to demand money from Sankpana or to stop making the akara. That was when she decided to go to Orunmila for divination at which she was told to serve Èsù with he-goat, 21 cowries, and akara. She made the sacrifice.

The next time she prepared akara, Sankpana collected the entire production and distributed them to divine priests, after which he asked each of them to pay. After collecting the money from them, he handed them over to the woman. The amount was more than all her previous losses.

When it appears at Ugbodu, the person should serve Èsù with he-goat, 21 cowries and akara. At divination, the person should serve ogun with a tortoise and Èsù with pigeon.

Chapter **11**

OWANRIN-IRETE
OWANRIN-AKIKO
OWANRIN-AREEGE

```
 I    II
 I    II
II     I
 I     I
```

He Made Divination for The Cock Before Marrying The Hen:

Igi gagara, okute gagara, adifa fun akiko magalaja ti'nshe
oko areege.

That was the Awo who made divination for the cock when he was going to take the hen for a wife. The cock was told to make sacrifice because he was going to compete with other suitors. He made the sacrifice with rat, fish, eko, akara, and a duck. Thereafter, he approached the hen with a proposal for marriage. The hen's parents however stipulated a condition for giving her away in marriage. The condition was for the prospective spouse to dig ridges in their farm. The first suitor to complete his ridging was to be the hen's husband.

Incidentally, the hen had already fallen in love with the cock. On the day appointed for the contest, the cock got to the farm to discover that the other contestants had already started digging. After waiting for the cock to show up, the hen began to cry:-

Areege oko mi si ko - Areege,
Erin oma mi a moke
Efon oma mi moke - Areege.
Areege oko mi si ko-o-Areege.

She was hailing on the cock as the spouse she preferred to show up before the elephant and the buffalo beat him in the ridging contest. When the cock heard the voice of the hen, he quickly left for the farm and commenced his own ridging. In no time, the cock had met and surpassed the other contestants. When the buffalo saw that the cock was beating everybody, he repeated an incantation which made the hoe being used by the cock to break up. Nonetheless, the cock raced home for another hoe. Once again he was ahead of everybody. When the elephant discovered that the cock was becoming unbeatable, he conjured the blade of the cock's hoe to split up. Once again, the cock hurried home to fetch a third hoe. As he was running back to the farm, the cock met Èsù, in the guise of an old woman, who advised him that if anyone disrupted him with any incantation, he should respond by saying :

"Tike Tike ni ikun mu arugboonro".

and that with those words, nothing would happen to his hoe. Thereafter, the cock reached the farm and continued his ridging. In no time, he had once more beaten the elephant. As he was passing the elephant, the latter began another incantation and the cock repeated his own anti-dotal incantation; and his hoe did not break anymore.

He was the first to finish digging his ridge and he hung his hoe on a stump to indicate that he had finished. As soon as the cock won the race, the hen went to embrace him, and the other contestants began to pursue them with sticks and cudgels. He however won the hands of the hen in marriage forever.

When it appears at divination, the person should be told to make sacrifice if he or she is proposing to marry someone, because other rivals would fight him or her to the finish.

He Made Another Divination for The Cock:

After he was finally married to the hen, the cock's enemies did not leave him alone. His handsomeness and melodious voice created lots of envy for him. His enemies eventually prepared medicine to make him develop leprosy. When they eventually touched him with the medicine, instead of developing into leprosy, it gave him the red crown on his head. When he came out the following morning, people began to wonder where and how he came by the beautiful crown on his head.

Since the enemies were not prepared to give up on him, they prepared another medicine for him to be sleepwalking. When he woke up the following morning, the medicine turned into shoes on his feet. Once again, his enemies began to wonder how he got the lovely sandals that were making him to be swaggering. Far from sleepwalking, he began to look more dignified and re-spectable.

Meanwhile, the enemies prepared medicine to cause elephantiasis for him. When he woke up the following morning, two beautiful feathers on his anus emerged. It is called irere in Yorùbá and ariokpa in Bini. That made him to become the cynosure of all eyes and the centre of attraction.

When God saw how the cock was being badgered by his enemies, the Almighty Father sent for him. When he appeared before God, He gave him the ASE to be announcing the dawn of the day to mark the beginning of His morning bath. With the ASE, God bestowed on the cock the authority to declare the day open, which made him to become even more famous, and he came to have many wives.

After receiving the ASE from God, he went to thank Orunmila who made divination and sacrifice for him. At that point, Orunmila advised him to make another sacrifice by serving his head with coconut and white kola nuts. He told him to serve his head privately without anyone being present. When he got home, instead of serving his head in secret as he was told to do, he invited a crowd to the ceremony. As the feasting was going on, the cock became drunk, and began to pass out excreta from his anus in the presence of his invites. That made the invites to abandon the ceremony. All his wives left him, with the exception of the hen, who stayed by him.

When his enemies saw that the hen stayed with him, they contrived another calamity for him. In the small hours of the morning, the enemies set fire to his house. The wife alerted him to the advent of war on their doorsteps. He was however able to fetch water to put out the fire. When the enemies saw that the fire was being extinguished, they launched an attack with cudgels and cutlasses, but he fought back by plucking out the eyes of each of his attackers. After they saw that he was fighting back fiercely, they ran away, only to recharge for another attack.

The last attack on him was to flood his house with water. This time, he lamented that this last battle was a more difficult one to combat. He decided to take refuge by flying to the roof of his house from where he saw that God was about to have his bath. He eventually crowed out the words:

Oja kekere hon-oo-ho

Meaning:

It is difficult to live in a place where people do not love themselves.

That has remained the call sign of the cock for signifying the dawn of a new day, ever since. With that he escaped from heaven to take refuge in the world.

When this Ifa appears at Ugbodu, the person will be told that he is surrounded by enemies, and that people are doing diabolical charms to create problems for him. He will have three difficult tests, but should serve his head with coconut and white kola nuts while backing his Ifa shrine, but alone and strictly privately, after everybody have slept. He should also serve Ogun with cock and tortoise.

When it appears at divination, the person should serve; his head with a cock, Ogun with tortoise, and Èsù with he-goat after bathing on Èsù shrine with discardable dresses, shoes and cap, which would be removed and deposited on the shrine. Three days later, the clothes, shoes and cap should be burnt on the shrine of Èsù.

With sacrifice, he will survive all the machinations of his enemies, and all the wickedness done to him, will become blessings in disguise. That was how the saying began:

Ika tiwon fi she akuko adiye,
Oda bi ewa la ra re

Meaning:

All the wickedness contrived to undo the cock, turned to instruments of elegance for him.

He Made Divination for Cockroach, Earthworm and The Hen:

Owanrin rere, Irete rere, made divination for the cockroach, the earthworm, and the hen, when they were all friends. Incidentally, the cockroach and the earthworm later teamed up against the hen. The two of them planned to be disturbing the hen from sleeping in the night. They began to tickle the body of the hen whenever she was asleep, thus preventing her from sleeping. The hen began to cry in the night whenever she was being disturbed. In the morning, the hen would complain about her experience to her two friends, the cockroach and the earthworm, who would instantly pretend to sympathize with her.

When the disturbance was becoming unbearable, the hen went to Orunmila for divination, at which she was advised not to reveal her experience to friends and not to trust any friends. She was told however to make sacrifice with ground pepper, sasswood (obo in Yorùbá and iyin in Bini) potassium permanganate (kaun) and dust. She produced the materials and the sacrifice was prepared for her to sprinkle round her house in the quiet hours of the night before going to bed.

The hen performed the operation after biding good night to her friends, who for once she did not take into confidence on the matter. When the cockroach and the earthworm later moved to enter the hen's house, they were caught up by the toxic effect of the preparation she sprinkled round her house and the two assailants died instantly.

The hen woke up in the morning to find the corpses of her two friends, after having been killed by the effect of the sacrifice she made. She then shouted. "Ewa wo o o Ala bu reke reke." From then on the hen vowed that the offspring of her iniquitous friends, would become food for herself and her children. That is why fowls feed on the cockroach and the earthworm whenever they come across them.

When this Ifa appears at divination, the person will be told that his/her problems are being caused by two very close friends who belong to the club of witchcraft. He or she should neither trust nor confide in friends. He or she should in any event proceed to make sacrifice quietly.

He Also Made Divination for The Cock When Befriending Èsù:

The cock had been advised at divination to desist from friendship with Èsù because he was going to be the loser in the end. He was also advised to make sacrifice with all edible foodstuffs, but he considered it unnecessary, since he could not imagine how Èsù, his bosom friend, could do anything against him. He was too naive to appreciate that Èsù has an unlimited capacity for mischief.

Meanwhile, the cock was invited by Èsù to accompany him to Orunmila's place for divination. When Orunmila sounded Ifa for the cock, Owanrin-Irete came out. The cock was advised that a close friend was about to get him into trouble for failing to make sacrifice. Once again, the cock was too simplistic to believe that Èsù was capable of harming him.

No sooner did they leave Orunmila's place than Èsù began to ask him the name of the Ifa that appeared for him at divination. The cock replied that it was Owanrin-Irete.

Thereafter, Èsù put the question repeatedly to the cock until the cock became thoroughly disgusted with his friends's behavior. When they got to the market, Èsù once again put the question to the cock, which made the latter to be so paranoid that he shouted the reply at the top of his voice; Owanrin-rete rete o ah! three times.

Since it is traditionally forbidden for the cock to crow in the market, the three occasions in which he repeated Owanrin-rete rete amounted to a crow. The people of the market in consonance with tradition, immediately apprehended the cock and beheaded him.

When this Ifa appears at divination, the person will be advised to serve Èsù with a big he-goat without any delay, to avoid the risk of sudden death which will be caused by a very close friend. If the Ifa appears at Ugbodu, the person should be advised to refrain forever from eating cock, and should under no circumstances serve his Ifa with a cock.

The Divination Made for Him When Leaving Heaven:

Owanrin re re re, Irete re re re, were the two Awos who made divination for Orunmila when he was coming from heaven. He was told that he was going to play a remarkable role in the world and as such should make sacrifice with:- a ram, a hen, snails, rat, fish, and pigeon to his guardian angel, while inviting all available Ifa priests; a he-goat to Èsù, adding rat and fish; and a white cock, a piece of white cloth, white chalk and white kola nuts to Olokun. He made all the sacrifices before leaving for the world. The sacrifice to his guardian angel lasted for seven days. Olokun promised to link up with him at a point in his life when he would become hopelessly despondent.

On getting to earth, he was thoroughly disappointed to see that life on earth was devoid of purpose and direction. He tried his utmost to make life a little more meaningful, but the more he tried, the greater the frustration he suffered. When he saw that he was making no headway, he decided to return to heaven to make more adequate preparations. Meanwhile, Èsù went to remind his guardian angel and Olokun of the elaborate sacrifices made to them by Owanrin-Irete before leaving for earth, and reported that the man had become so disillusioned that he was at the point of returning to heaven.

Olokun reacted by sending one of his daughters to rendezvous with him in the market. Back on earth, he had finalized arrangements for his return trip to heaven on the market day. As he was about to leave for heaven from the market, he met a woman dressed in immaculate white outfit. The woman greeted him and he responded. He was dressed in the full regalia of an Ifa priest. When the woman asked him where he was going, he replied that he had become so disappointed about the emptiness of life on earth that he had decided to return to heaven. The woman shocked him by telling him that she came from heaven to meet him, and that she was going to wait for him until he returned from heaven. He was so taken aback by the overtures of the woman that he decided to delay his departure to heaven.

At the same time, Èsù transfigured into an elderly Ifa priest to advise him to proceed with his plans to return to heaven and not be disturbed by the transitory attractions of a woman. With that, he bade adieu to the woman and left for heaven. On his arrival in heaven, he went to see the two Awos who had previously made divination for him. After divination, he was told to approach his guardian angel and Olokun, to ask them why they had forsaken him so helplessly on earth. The Awos however told him that Olokun's daughter had already met him on earth without recognizing her, which made him to surmise that she was probably the woman he met on his way to heaven.

The Awos told him to serve his Ifa, Olokun and Èsù as soon as he returned to earth.

While he was away several men made amorous overtures to Olokun's daughter, but she re-buffed them by saying that she was expecting her husband. On his return journey from heaven, he again met the woman in the market. After welcoming him, she offered to follow him home. As soon as he got to his house, she complained that the place required a facelift.

Unknown to him, the woman had a large retinue that accompanied her from heaven. The following morning her followers arrived to give the house a white renovation. He was now certain that Olokun had finally come into his life. From then on, her followers were bringing wares from heaven for sale on every market day and the family soon became affluent.

On one market, she proposed that the two of them should go to the market together. People were surprised to know that the paragon of Venusian elegance and excellence had opted to marry Orunmila. They were hailed all the way to, in and from, the market. Not long afterwards, she became pregnant, but he had forgotten about the three sacrifices he was advised in heaven to make as soon as he returned to the world. His memory had completely been obfuscated by the unparalleled demonstration of genuine love from his wife. It was when he made divination for the incoming child that he was eventually reminded of the debt of sacrifices that he owed. He was told that the incoming child was going to be greater than his parents.

He was advised to give white cock, white cloth, white chalk, white kola nuts and parrot's feather to Olokun. As soon as he collected these materials, his wife told him that they belonged to her and he surrendered them to her. Thereafter, he gave a ram to his Ifa in the presence of several Ifa priests. At the same time, he gave a he-goat to Èsù. All the sacrifices lasted for seven days. In the fullness of time, the woman gave birth to a child who turned out to be money. The child became so popular that nobody paid attention to his parents anymore. Everybody took to the child and cherished him. Orunmila was eventually invited by the king to be his second-in-command. He lived to a ripe old age in peace and prosperity.

When this Ifa appears at Ugbodu, the person will be assured that a woman will come to transform his life and that the woman will give birth to a child, who will be more famous than his parents.

He Made Divination for The River and The Sea:

He advised the Sea to serve his head with a white goat, 2 pieces of coconuts and white kola nuts and to invite people when making the sacrifice and also to give a he-goat to Èsù. He was advised to provide plenty of drinks to entertain his invites. He was however told that after serving his head, he should no longer participate in anybody else's head-serving ceremony. He quickly made the sacrifices, to which he invited all divine priests, and they all responded positively. He was however advised not to drink on the day he served his head.

All the rivers were also advised by Orunmila to serve their heads. They did not serve their heads before going to assist the sea in serving his own head. It was only the lake who served his head after which he did not honor the sea's invitation. That is why the lake is independent of the sea and the rivers to this day.

After the ceremony at the Sea's (Olokun's) house, all the rivers became drunk, and unwittingly, they all moved towards the direction of the Sea. That is why all rivers owe allegiance to Olokun and flow in towards the sea.

When this Ifa appears at Ugbodu and the special sacrifice (ono-Ifa of odiha) is being performed, the sand is collected from the source of the river and dried to be used as the Iyerosun for marking the odu. Cowries are also ground to be added to the sand. The traditional Iyerosun is not used.

He Made Divination for The Magician Called Agamurere:

Igi gagara, okute gagara. Adifa fun Agamurere, onlo she
Awo fun Ologunmare.

He made divination for Agamurere, the magician, when he was going to challenge a more experienced mystic called Ologungunmare. He was advised to give a cock and a tortoise to Èsù before going because the man he was going to challenge, was much stronger than himself. He did not see any need to make sacrifice because he relied heavily on his magical powers.

When he got to Ologungunmare's house, he demonstrated several magical feats, but his performances were effectively checkmated by his host. When he transfigured into a rat, Ologungunmare turned into a cat, ready to swallow the rat. When he turned into a ram, Ologungunmare turned into a tiger. After the contest Ologungunmare told him that he had to return home to acquire more esoteric skills before coming back to challenge him.

When he returned home, he went to Orunmila for fresh divination. Orunmila reminded him of the sacrifice he failed to make. Orunmila advised him to make the sacrifice before returning to challenge Ologungunmare, but this time he had to make the sacrifice with a he-goat. He warned that the consequences could be fatal if he did not make the sacrifice. In spite of the premonition, he returned to challenge Ologungunmare once more, without making the sacrifice.

On getting there, he demonstrated new feats and the man he challenged stood to watch him. He brought his performances to crescendo when he suspended himself in the air and began to dance in the air without his feet touching the ground. He climaxed his performances by severing his head from his body while both parts continued to dance in the air. That was the point at which Ologungunmare turned into a giant eagle, flew up high into the air and captured the severed head of Agamurere, and flew into the air with it. When Agamurere later sought to join his head to his body, his head was no where to be found. His body eventually fell to the ground, strayed headlessly into the forest to become an anthill.

When this odu appears at divination, the person should be advised not to rely too heavily on diabolical charms. He should arrange to have his own Ifa, because only Orunmila would help him to live long on earth, otherwise he is likely to die young.

Chapter **12**

OWANRIN-EKA
OWANRIN-WO-OKA
OWANRIN-ALA-AYOKA

```
II  II
I   II
II  I
II  I
```

He Made Divination for The Calabash Before Going To The Farm:

Owanrin woka woka, was the Ifa priest who made divination for the calabash, when she was going to the farm at the beginning of the farming year. She was advised to make sacrifice to forestall hostility from mankind and animals against herself and her children. She was advised to make sacrifice with a knife, he-goat, shea-butter (ori-oyo) cotton wool and bitter leaves. She made the sacrifice and subsequently went to the farm.

When she germinated, Esu brought out the cotton wool with which she made sacrifice to conceal her identity and to prevent people and animals from feeding on her foliage. The Ifa priest had prepared a noxious serum for her to use in rubbing the bodies of her children before exposing them to the world. When men and animals sampled the fruits of the calabash, unlike those of her sister, the melon, they were very toxic and bitter. People then left her children alone to mature. When the children were matured enough for harvesting, the knife with which she made sacrifice was used to cut them up nicely for use in fetching and storing water, palm oil and palm wine. Her smaller children were cut for use either as ornamental instruments or as plates for eating food. Upon realizing that sacrifice had brought her salvation, she sang in praise of the Awo, Owanrin-woka-woka, who made divination and sacrifice for her.

At divination, the Ifa priest can say that the divinee or someone close to him or her is making marriage proposals. Whoever is in that position should make sacrifice for the success of the marriage and for the survival of his or her children.

The Divination Made for Him Before Leaving Heaven:

Oloyo yo yo Lere, Oloyo yo yo (Happiness begets prosperity) was the Awo who made divination for this odu before coming to the world. He was advised to refrain from; being aggressive and temperamental and from drinking alcohol. He was told to make sacrifice with; the meat of cow, a goat, a hen, snail, rat and fish to his guardian angel; all the materials for serving Olokun including, white cock, white pigeon, white eagle's feather, red parrot's feather and maracas (sekere or ukuse), and a he-goat to Esu. He left for the world after making the sacrifices.

In consonance with his destiny, he became a trader on getting to the world, but he did not serve Olokun on earth as he did in heaven. When his trading business was not yielding impressive profits, he went for divination during which he was told to have his Olokun fully prepared in addition to his Ifa. He made the sacrifice with white cock and white pigeon and prepared the Olokun shrine close to his Ifa shrine. Before the following morning, he found a divination instrument on his Olokun shrine, which he began to use for divination. While continuing with his trading business, it was divining that incipiently launched him into success which enabled him to marry many wives and to have many children. Subsequently, his wives took over the trading business while he devoted all his time to the worship of Orunmila and Olokun. The family eventually became very wealthy and he was given a chieftaincy title.

When this Ifa appears at Ugbodu, the person will be told to serve his Ifa with the meat of cow, hen, snail, rat and fish and to have his own Olokun, by asking Olokun priests to prepare a moulded Olokun image for his Ifa. He should prepare his Esu with a he-goat without any delay. If the special sacrifice is not prepared quickly, the person can easily become an idiot or a paranoiac.

He Made Divination for the Squirrel and the Boa:

The squirrel was so poor that he was having problems in feeding himself. He then went to Orunmila for divination and he was told to serve his head with kola nuts and to serve Esu with palm fruits. It was Esu that subsequently introduced the palm fruits and other fruits to the squirrel as nutritious food for him to be eating.

At the same time, the boa (oka in Yorùbá and arumwoto in Bini) also went for divination, and Orunmila told him to make sacrifice very quickly because, enemies were searching for him to kill. He was told to serve his head quietly and secretly, under a thicket without the knowledge of anyone and not to allow anyone to punctuate his prayers with "Amen."

Meanwhile, the Oba of the town had been told to serve his Ifa with a boa and he had issued orders for one to be procured for him by all means. That coincided with the time when the boa was going to serve his head to avoid sudden death. Instead of serving his head at night in accordance with tradition, he preferred to do it in broad day light. Unknown to him, the harbinger appointed by God to herald the presence of the boa (the squirrel) was around when he went under the thicket to serve his head. As soon as the boa started serving his head, the squirrel began to interrupt his prayers with ASE, ASE, ASE, O, Oka-elewu-obobo (that is, Amen to the prayers of the velvet skinned boa). The words of the squirrel alerted passersby who were already combing the forest for the boa. They immediately cleared the thicket, found the boa and tied him up to be taken to the palace, where the Oba used him to serve his Ifa, after which peace returned to his kingdom.

When this Ifa appears at Ugbodu, the person should be advised to beware of a talkative friend. Before the completion of the Ifa ceremony, a pregnant woman will come in. She should be told to serve Ifa with a boa because Orunmila is going to do her a favor.

The owner of the Ifa will serve Esu with a squirrel, akara and Eko. At ordinary divination, the person should be advised to serve Esu with a he-goat, and to serve his head with a pigeon to avert the trouble that a friend will create for him.

He Made Divination for Oro When He Was Travelling:

Owanrin woka woka, Awo oro, odifa fun Oro nijo t'onsha'wo
lo so'de Egba. Ani ki Oro ru ebo, Agutan l'onfi she'bo.

He made divination for Oro when he was going to practice Awo in Egba land. He was told to make sacrifice with a female sheep. He made the sacrifice and went to the place. On getting there he won the admiration and confidence of his clients and returned home with lots of gifts and plenty of money.

When it appears at divination for someone preparing for a business tour, he should be advised to make sacrifice in order to gain benefits, honor and respect in the place.

The Divination He Made To Save His Son From Death:

Emo lo lo ro oju okpo. Efi lawo ilogi jan, ebe lambe
Orunmila ko to ja ewe alariku han eni. Adafa fun Ayeghe
igbo t'inshe omo bibi agboniregun. Ebo ariku lo ma ru-o.

The rats are the eyes of the roof of a house. One has to beg Orunmila to show one the life-saving leaves in the bush, were the Awos who made divination for the son of Orunmila when death was threatening him. He was told to make sacrifice with a he-goat, rat, fish and snail.

He made the sacrifice, and the son was rescued from the hands of death.

When this Ifa appears as Ayeo at divination and death is portended, the above sacrifice should be recommended.

A Second Sacrifice To Save His Son From Death:

Elete lete nye. Omoran la mu oro'lo .Okete to
ja ole eyin lo fi ile ara re han iku. Adafa fun Orunmila
t'onlo gba omo re si le lowo uku.

Only the thinker knows what he is thinking. It is the expert who is asked how to do what he knows. The rabbit who stole palm fruits and left them at the entrance to his hole, shows the entrance to his house to death. These were the Awos who made divination for Orunmila when he was going to rescue his son from the cold hands of death. He made sacrifice with a he-goat, cock, fish and rat. After the sacrifice, his son survived the wrath of death.

When it appears at divination, the person will be advised not to accommodate any lodging visitor for the time being, in order to avert the risk of being harmed by his enemies through the visitor. He should however make sacrifice to forestall such an eventuality.

Chapter **13**

OWANRIN-ETURUKPON
OWANRIN-OJUKOTO

```
 ||  ||
 ||  ||
 |   |
 ||  |
```

He Made Divination for Four Children of The Same Father:

The tortoise, the snail, the squirrel and the boa were born of the same father by different mothers. Their father lived to a ripe old age before he died. The snail was a farmer, the boa was a hunter, the tortoise was a confidence trickster, and the squirrel was an itinerant traditional doctor who was always travelling away from home. The squirrel was therefore away on a business trip when his father died. On the demise of their father, the three home-based brothers went to Orunmila for divination and they were told to make sacrifice to ward off the wrath of their junior brother who was away from home. They were told to serve Esu with a he-goat. Since they could not envisage any danger from the innocuous squirrel, they did not consider it necessary to make the sacrifice.

Their father had three garments which were shared among the three home-based brothers after the burial. The snail got the iron dress (alitikaka) the tortoise got the stone dress (alatikoko) while the boa got the velvet garment (ewu obobo guenren). There was no dress left for the squirrel who was not at home.

Three years after the death of their father, the squirrel returned home from his tour. After performing his funeral rights, he asked for his share of his father's legacy and he was told to get lost. When he got to his father's grave, he found a fly whisk on top of it and took it, which is what he uses to cover his tail, to this day.

When he got to the forest the following day, God called him and appointed him as the crier to be heralding the presence of the boa for killing the rabbit, who was God's own servant. With his newly acquired instrument of authority, the squirrel vowed to be chanting the death knell against his three brothers wherever he found them.

He began by looking for the boa whose presence, he was specifically appointed by God to herald. As soon as he sighted the boa in his traditional habitat of the thicket, the squirrel began his battle cry:

Oka gbe ewu obobo geunren,
Aghun gbe ewu alatikoko,
Aghun gbe ewu alatikaka,

Ode wa wo o oka o, elewu obobo,
kia kia kia kia.

He was drawing the hunter's attention to the presence of the boa in the vicinity. The hunter immediately cut a pointed stick with which he pierced the head of the boa to the ground before beheading him. The squirrel meted out similar punishments to the snail and the tortoise.

That is why anytime the squirrel is chanting his battle-cry, it is an indication the boa, or the tortoise or the snail is around.

When this Ifa appears at Ugbodu, the person will be advised to make sacrifice in his home base (idile in Yorùbá and Igiogbe in Bini) at the shrine of their ancestors with a goat, because of some wrong he did there in his present life or at a previous incarnation. He should forbid sharing from any legacy, but if he cannot avoid it, he should first serve Esu with a he-goat before participating in it. At divination, the person should serve Esu with a he-goat and Ifa with a hen, fly-whisk (oroke) or horse tail, and maracas (sekere or ukuse).

Divination for Three Brothers:

Eni ti ebi n kpa oun loto oju ule olo jule kiri.
Bi ko ba she dana dana a'nshe doni doni.
Eni ti oba shoro oun lo kan eyin ilekun.
Adafa fun Onikporo, abufun Onitaji, atunda fun
Obokun t'inshe omo ikeyin won lenje lenje.
Awon meteta lo'de okun eye.

It is the hungry loafer who strays from house to house.
If he is not a robber, he is a flirt in search of sensual
satisfaction.
It is the guilty-conscious person that hides behind the door.

These were the Awos who made divination for Onikporo, Onitaji and Obokun, the youngest of the three brothers. The three of them went to the bush to set traps for catching birds. They returned home after setting the traps.

The following morning, the two most senior brothers went to check the traps. Obokun could not go with them. Incidentally, it was only Obokun's traps that caught birds. They removed the birds from the traps, but on getting home they lied that it was their own traps that caught the birds. When Obokun subsequently went to the bush, he saw all the indications that it was his traps that caught the birds brought home by his elder brothers. On getting home, he accused his brothers of cheating because he saw no sign to confirm that it was their traps that caught the birds they brought home. A quarrel ensued between the three brothers, which was remitted to the elders for settlement. The elders sent two verifiers to the bush to see whose traps caught which birds.

After inspecting all the traps, the verifiers were satisfied that it was Obokun's traps that caught the birds. When they reported their findings to the elders, the two brothers were accused of stealing and ordered to surrender the birds to Obokun.

When it appears at divination, the person should be advised to take proper care of his property and should not leave his valuable belongings under the care of other people, to obviate the risk of being deprived of them.

He Made Divination for The Divine Priest:

Iyan o da tun ngun. Obe o da tun she,
Ogun lo ba oda tun ro. Adafa fun Alaworo ti oun ti eko lori.
The pounded yam did not pound properly and had to be re-pounded.
The soup was also not properly cooked and required further cooking.
The battle fought for Oba had to be fought again.

These were the Awos who made divination for the divine priest, who was told that the sacrifice he made previously did not manifest because it was not done with the appropriate materials. He was required to repeat the sacrifice with a sheep to the divinity he was serving. He was advised to do it in order to live to a ripe old age in good health and prosperity.

When it appears at divination, the person will be told that the sacrifice he made was not accepted and will be told to repeat it. He or she should be asked what divinity he or she is serving. That divinity should be served with the appropriate animal or bird - details to be probed by the diviner.

Divined for Ogun and Other Divinities:

Ogun ni ikin Owanrin. Eta-dogbon ni ikin Eturukpon.
Adifa fun Ogun, abufun omo erumole gbogbo nijo ti won
ti lo ke orun bo wa si kole aye. Gbogbo won toro oju
omo Orisa. Ani ki won ru ebo.

The Ifa seeds of Owanrin (that is, the number of Ikin on the right side) numbered twenty, and those of Eturukpon (the number of Ikin on the left) numbered twenty-seven. Those were the names of the Awos who made divination for Ogun and all the other divinities when they were coming to the world. They all went to request for esoteric vision from God. They were told to make sacrifice with a hen and a pigeon. Ogun, Olokun, Sàngó and Osanyin were the only ones who made the sacrifice. That is why they are the only divinities endowed with extra-perceptual vision, and why their priests divine by possession, which makes it impossible for them to see what is simultaneously happening in heaven and on earth.

When it appears at divination, the person will be advised to make sacrifice on account of a contest he is scheduled to have with other people, most probably in his place of work. He will win it if he makes sacrifice.

The Divination He Made Before Leaving Heaven:

Owanrin le gon gon gon. Eturukpon titu kpese, were the two Awos who made divination for this odu when he was coming to the world. He was advised to make sacrifice to; his guardian angel with goat, hen, rat and fish; Esu with he-goat, corn yam, plantain, garden eggs and pepper; and his head with a cock on the eve of his departure, while sitting on an elevated seat or throne. He did all the sacrifices after which he obtained God's blessing before leaving for the world. He was advised to take to farming when he got to the world.

Contrary to the advice at divination, he took to Ifa practice and completely neglected farming. He however made no headway as an Ifa priest, because he could neither afford to marry and have children; nor to build a house of his own. When he finally went to other Ifa priests for divination, his own odu appeared, and he was told that he was getting no where in his life because he had strayed away from the path of his destiny. He was told to serve his head on top of a hill in the forest after giving a he-he-goat to Esu, adding yams, corn, plantain, pepper and garden eggs.

After eating his he-goat, Esu went to the spot where Orunmila served his head the previous day and set the place on fire. It burnt the bush so effectively that Esu also subsequently went to make it a farm by planting all the crops with which Orunmila had made sacrifice to him. The crops began to germinate while Orunmila was still engaged in his Ifa practice.

Meanwhile, the Hare was the first to visit the farm where she began to uproot the corn planted therein. When Esu saw what the Hare was doing, he arrested her and accused her of stealing. The Hare begged for forgiveness, but Esu insisted on dragging her to the owner of the farm. The Hare was a very beautiful lady. When she was brought before Orunmila with a charge of stealing from his farm, he was dumbfounded because he did not know of any farm he had cultivated. Esu however improvised his bearings by telling him that the farm was made for him by his guardian angel, following the sacrifice he made to Esu and his head. Orunmila went to the forest to see a massive expanse of farm fully cultivated, supposedly belonging to him.

Since the penalty for stealing was death, the Hare offered herself in marriage to Orunmila. He agreed and began to live with her as man and wife. After thanking Esu with another he-goat, Orunmila began to work on the farm.

When it was time for harvesting corn, Esu made sure that all those who planted corn in the town had very poor harvests, so much so that maize was only available in Orunmila's farm. Meanwhile, the Parrot was combing the area for corn to feed on. When she finally came across Orunmila's farm, she began to feed on the corn. Once again, Esu got her arrested and arraigned before Orunmila. Having put her feet down, the parrot could not fly up again and so agreed to live with Orunmila as a second wife.

Thereafter, the two wives were working on his farm while he was continuing with his Ifa practice, in which he was now having a wide clientele. At the same time, there was famine in the community on account of the poor harvest of that year. Seeing that Orunmila's was the only farm that yielded a prolific harvest, people began to steal food crops from his farm. His wives were however apprehending the thieves and were bringing them before their husband. Overtime, Orunmila came to have 201 servants living with him. He was subsequently able to build a bigger house and his servants were doing the farming chores.

After prosperity had come to him, he was made the Oba of the town. Thereafter, he gave a thanksgiving feast to the community during which he sang in praise of the Awos who made divination and sacrifice for him. He reigned in peace and prosperity and lived to a ripe old age.

When this Ifa appears at Ugbodu, the person will be advised to prepare an elevated throne for his Ifa. His profession will have something to do with farming or agriculture.

He Made Divination for The People of Benin:

Apa awo won lo'de asorin
Ogbe ni awo won ni ilu Iroda
Ope teere eti ilode.

These were the Ifa priests who made divination for the people of Benin. They were advised to make sacrifice in order to have a genuine love for one another. They refused to make the sacrifice. That is why they love outsiders (non-Binis) more than they love themselves and why they do not forgive one another when offended.

That is why Orunmila says that the people of Benin do not exclaim twice, only once "heu or eeh or huu;" and remember to offer gratitude for previous gratification, unless when coming to ask for a new favor.

When this Odu appears at divination, the person will be told that he is very selfish and that if he must prosper, he should learn to have good feelings towards others, so that God would in turn have time for him. He should make sacrifice with a cock, yam, corn, beans and plantain.

Chapter **14**

OWANRIN-OSE
OWANRIN-SEKPERE
OWANRIN-WESE
OWANRIN-'DA-'SENA

```
 I   II
II   II
 I    I
II    I
```

The Divination Made for Him Before Leaving Heaven:

Okiti Sekpere, Awo eba ono, was the Awo who made divination for this odu when he was coming from heaven. He was told to make elaborate sacrifices to deter the risk of having a very difficult time on earth. He vowed in heaven to make wickedness his stock-in-trade while on earth. He was told that if he was to thrive in wickedness, he should make sacrifices to; Esu with a he-goat; his guardian angel with multicolored hen, tortoise, goat and white cloth; and the Awos to make special sacrifice for him with four pigeons, white and red kola nuts, rags and crushed yam. He was to go to the footpath to serve his head with one pigeon to the right, and another pigeon to the left of the foot path after having a bath on the foot path with leaves to be prepared by the Ifa priest.

He was so scared by the size and intricacies of the sacrifice that he bluntly refused to make any of them. He then came to the world where he began to practice as an Ifa priest. He was fond of making predictions at divination that he knew stood no chance of manifesting. In spite of that, he became notorious for demanding extortionate fees for his services. Esu was also equally determined to frustrate him because he got no where. Nobody ever came to him a second time for divination, because he never did anything that turned out satisfactorily. At a point, after he had become known as a quack, nobody went to him any more for divination. When he realized that he was a failure, he decided to return to heaven for better preparations.

On getting to heaven, he went to the same Awo who had previously divined for him. The Awo reminded him of the sacrifice he failed to make, and his guardian angel warned him that it was no use returning to the world without making the sacrifices. Once again, he threw up his hands in despair, saying he had no money to fund the elaborate sacrifices.

When he returned to the world without making sacrifice, nobody paid heed to him because he had been written off as a charlatan. He eventually gave up Ifa practice for farming. He was also a complete failure in farming and he lived a life of despicable poverty to the end of his life.

When this Ifa appears at Ugbodu, the person should be advised to make the elaborate sacrifices which the odu refused to make in heaven, failing which, he would be a hard-luck case. It is an unfortunate odu and it will take a lot of sacrifices to remove the stigma of failure from his destiny. If it appears at ordinary divination, the person should be advised to go to his family home to revoke a curse on him from a previous incarnation. If the Ifa appears at divination for a reasonably successful person, he will be forewarned not to associate with a hard luck person.

He Made Divination for The Farmer:

Owanrin-Wese babalawo Nomo, odifa fun Nomo t'in she Ogbe ni jo t'oure lo ilu almo.

He made divination for Nomo, the farmer when he was travelling to an unknown place. He was told to serve Esu with a he-goat, but he refused to do it. Rather, he preferred to travel out of his town into the unknown. He traveled with his cutlass in hand. He was apparently fed up with life and had ceased to worry about his safety. After traveling for sometime, he came across a crippled man with one hand and one leg.

The man told him to stand still and listen to him, but he was in no mood to listen to anyone, let alone a seemingly helpless cripple. The cripple however told him that he would come across a pipe loaded with tobacco in front. He advised him to smoke the pipe back to meet him.

Not long afterwards, he saw the pipe loaded with tobacco. He took it and as soon as he started smoking it, he began to walk back to meet the cripple not knowing what to expect. As soon as he met the cripple, he requested Nomo to take him to his house. Reluctantly, Nomo agreed to take him to his house.

On getting home the cripple told Nomo not to go outside the house until further notice. Not even to his farm or the market. The following day, the man asked for food. Nomo snapped back by querying how he expected him to get food to provide, when he was not supposed to leave the house. The cripple retorted by telling him to go to the back of the house to collect the yams deposited there. The man told him that he only ate white and palm-oiled crushed yam (ewo or Obobo). He went to the back of the house and collected the yams he found there. Nomo's next problem was who was going to cook the yam. Once again, the cripple told him to give one of the yams to a woman on the kitchen to do the cooking. Upon meeting an unknown woman in the kitchen, Nomo began to wonder about the identity of his visitor.

Nomo was given to going out in the night. One night, the cripple told Nomo to carry him to the venue of a meeting that was going to be held that night. Nomo did as he was told. On getting to a spot, the cripple told him to put him down and return home but not to leave the house until the following morning, when he was to come back to take him. The man emphasized that he should not leave the house for any reason whatsoever for the rest of the night.

Nomo returned home all right, but could not resist the curiosity to find out what the man was going to do. No sooner did he reach home therefore, than he took off again for the venue of the meeting. On getting there, he met a large gathering, but was dumbfounded to see the 'cripple' standing firmly on his two legs using his supposedly lame hand to feed someone who was apparently the king of the night. The 'cripple' was moving swiftly all over the place.

After spying on all the goings-on at the meeting, he decided to return home but before he could set out for the return journey one young man at the meeting called Asisenren called on Nomo to come to the meeting and take a seat. As soon as he got to the meeting, he was accused of spying. The 'cripple' told the king of the night that he had warned Nomo not to return until the following morning, but that he had allowed his curiosity to overwhelm his senses. He was given a summary trial and sentenced to be turned into a goat, he was beheaded, and his corpse was pounded and used for preparing idabo (uhumwum ewe no rie 'we in Bini). That is the head of the goat that eats other goats, and which is present at all properly solemnized and completed Ifa shrines. It sees all that goes on during an Ifa ceremony, but lacks the mouth to reveal what it sees. Iyerosun represents all the people that Nomo saw at that nocturnal meeting. In Ifa parlance, it is called amidikuku.

When it appears at Ugbodu, the person should be warned not to insist on seeing what he is not supposed to see, and that he should refrain from night outing and from joining any meeting.

At divination, the person should serve Esu with a he-goat before travelling or going to where he has been invited. If he goes without making the sacrifice, he will not return.

Divined for Orungun, The Father of Adedeji:

Ewe odan bale oro kpelenje kplenje. Ewe ogugu ba le gbandu gbanko.
Adafa fun orogun baba
Adedeji ti a ni koma ja koro lo'gun .Ta ni ko ma ja igede ake,
ko ma ba sun lori ima, ki o ma ba
fi ago if'owo she omi mu. Ebo ni ko ru.

The leaves of the umbrella tree (odan in Yorùbá and obadab in Bini) fall down lightly. The leaves of another plant called ogugu drop heavily on the ground. These were the Awos who made divination for Orongun, the father of Adedeji, when he was advised to make sacrifice to avert the risk of being taken by surprise in a fight.

He was also advised to avoid; using destructive incantation; eating while standing on top of leaves; sleeping on palm leaves; and drinking water with cups made from white melon. That was at a time when he was having a dispute with a man with whom he belonged to the same cult.

If he fought relentlessly, he would be contravening the oath he took at the cult, and hence be undoing himself. He was told to make sacrifice with a he-goat. After doing the sacrifice, the Ifa priests advised him not to travel anywhere within a period of fourteen days, and not to compete for anything with anybody. He took heed of the instructions and was victorious over his opponent, because sacrifice like perseverance, does not fail to manifest in favor of those who do it.

When it appears at divination, the person should be advised not to use destructive charms against anybody no matter how much he has been provoked. He should not travel anywhere for a period of fourteen days and should not compete for anything with anybody, to prevent the danger of undoing himself.

The Divination Made for His Uncaring Wife

Bi obe ki ofun obe bu, lo ndifa fun akpetebi Orunmila, ta ni ko ma yo omi obe fun oko re. To ri ki Esu ma binu si.

Take soup with spoon and steer it - was the name of the Awo who made divination for the wife of Orunmila when she was using spoon to shift the condiments of the soup to one side while giving the watery portion to her husband. She was forewarned that Esu was already annoyed over how she was treating her husband and would punish her unless she refrained from the abominable action. Her explanation was that she was doing so because she wanted the soup to last. Nonetheless, she was told not to economize on her husband's stomach. She made sacrifice with two rats, and the next day, Orunmila made sacrifice with two goats. She subsequently apologized for her misdeeds, promising to change for better behavior.

When it appears at divination for a woman, she should be told to refrain from maltreating her husband, lest Esu would punish her for it.

Special Preparation for Pregnancy By This Odu:

When a woman is anxiously desperate for a child, Orunmila advises that she will be told to make sacrifice with a rabbit and ginger seeds (ighere or iyere in Yorùbá and Oziza in Bini). After kneading them with the appropriate leaves, the paste is mixed with honey. The Ifa priest should then recite the apposite incantation to the effect that:

It is thorough menstruation that the rat, fish
birds, animals and women, become pregnant to
give birth to their young ones. That was how
God proclaimed it. I therefore invite the
Creator who made the proclamation to allow this
woman to become pregnant after using this special
medicament.

The woman will start leaking medicine as soon as she finishes her menstruation, throughout the month. If she meets her husband when applying the medicine, she will surely become pregnant.

Divination for The Man Suffering From Elephantiasis:

Owanrin-wese-wese ki ara omo gan-gan-gan, was the Awo who made divination for Olukunrun, when he was suffering from a disease that made his body to swell up disproportionately.

He was advised to make sacrifice with a rat called eku-oloyan, ashes, leaves called ewe-ofe and black soap. He produced the materials and the Ifa priest used them to prepare a soap dish for him to use in bathing daily. Within a period of seven days, the sickness abated and he became very happy and sang in praise of the Ifa priest.

Owanrin-wese-wese ki ara mo
Odifa fun Olukunrun ibule,
Ti on fi ojojumo wu ni ara.
Oni oun gbo riru ebo, oun ru,
Oun gbo eru etukesu, oun tu.
Koi pe, koi jina,
Ara wa le bi okuta.

Meaning:

Owanrin-Ose was the Awo who made divination
for Olukunrun, who was afflicted with a
dangerous disease,
That made his body to be swelling up every day.
He listened to the advice of the Ifa priest,
who told him to make sacrifice; and
he did it and soon became well.

When it appears at divination, the person will be told that he is developing an illness. He should make sacrifice to prevent it from becoming fatal.

Chapter **15**

OWANRIN-OFUN

```
II  II
I   II
II  I
I   I
```

The Divination He Made Before Leaving Heaven for Earth:

Wofun Wofun, Yenden yende, were the Awos who made divination for this odu when he was coming to the world. He was advised to make sacrifices to his guardian angel with a ram; Esu with a he-goat; and to feast the heavenly divinities with a goat, hen, cow meat and pigeon. The volume of the sacrifice scared him so much that he wanted to give up the idea of coming to the world. However, he subsequently raised a loan from Elenini the obstacle divinity, (Idoboo in Bini), to fund the sacrifice. Elenini however warned him not to forget to repay the loan when he got to the world.

When he got to the world, he became a high priest of the communal divinity of his town called (Umole Ilu) as well as a practicing Ifa priest. Meanwhile, Elenini was waiting in heaven for the repayment of his loan. Incidentally, Owanrin-Ofun did not prosper sufficiently to be able to repay the loan. He got married to a wife who could not produce a child. Seeing that he was not making it on earth, he returned to heaven for further preparations. As soon as he reached heaven, he was apprehended by Elenini, who instantly demanded the repayment of his loan. It was his guardian angel who came to his rescue, by raising money to repay Elenini. His guardian angel told him that he should take full-time to the worship of Umole Ilu of which he was the high priest, if he was to prosper on earth. He went to the guardian angel of Umole Ilu in heaven, to teach him its mode of worship. He was taught how to serve it and to begin by making sacrifice to him as soon as he returned to earth with; a cow, a goat, and a hen. The guardian angel of Umole-Ilu gave him the artifacts of the divinity to be placed at his shrine on earth. With that, he returned to the world.

On getting to the world, he made an announcement that every household in the town was required to contribute money to make a feast to Umole-Ilu. The contributions were accordingly made and the materials for the sacrifice were procured. After the sacrifice, prosperity returned to the town and to him. People began to have children and money flowed into the town from all directions. In accordance with the instructions given to him in heaven by the guardian angel of Umole-ilu, he caused a hut to be built in the bush where annual festivals were to commence before leading a procession to the town's shrine. He named the hut Ugbodumi or Ugbodu.

When this odu appears at divination, the person should be told to go and serve Odu, and it is only done by strong and adept Ifa priests. Only very few Ifa priests have it and know how to serve it. It is an ORO divinity shrouded in secrecy which women and non-initiates are not allowed to see.

Divined for The Town of Ewanrin-Ofu:

Age ku uta losh'una ke riri keriri loko ayiya.
Adifa fun won ni ewanrin ofu. Ebo itura ni ki won ru,
ki gra won ba'le.

The stump of Uta tree in the farm makes a glowing fire, was in the farm of a man called Ayiya. That was the name of the Awo who made divination for the people of the town called Ewanrin-ofu, when they had no peace of mind. He told them to make sacrifice with sixteen snails for peace and tranquility to return to them. They made the sacrifice and serenity returned to the town.

At divination, the person will be told that a settled life is eluding his family. They should make sacrifice for prosperity and tranquility. If the divinee is a man, he should be advised to have his own Ifa. If she is a woman, she should encourage her husband to have his own Ifa.

He Made Divination for Oro, When He Owed a Woman:

Owanrin wofun wofun, Awo Oro, odifa fun oro ni jo t'oun le
gbese egba efa lowo obinrin kon. Obinrin na bere si yo lenu.

He made divination for Oro when he was indebted to a woman to the tune of six bags of money. The woman was relentlessly demanding payment of the debt from Oro, so much that he could not venture to go outside his house due to the molestation. He decided subsequently to go to Orunmila for divination, where he was advised to make sacrifice with 3 rats, a thread and a knife. He made the sacrifice after which he was advised to be yelling whenever he was coming out at night. Traditionally, Oro does not come out in the daytime and women are not expected to see him when he bellows a curfew at night. He was assured that if he did as he was told the debt would lapse.

After the sacrifice, the woman was proposing to go to Oro's house to demand the payment of the debt, when she suddenly heard the following yell of a curfew:

Mema, Mema, Mema, Mema,
Mo ti shebo Owanrin wofun wofun.

As soon as the bawl of the curfew was heard, all women began to escape into their houses. The woman herself gave up her plans to go to Oro's house for fear of losing her life because of six bags of money. That was how Oro's debt to her lapsed into eternity.

At divination, the person should be told to make sacrifice to avoid embarrassment for a meagre indebtedness. If he makes the sacrifice, the debt will lapse.

His Divination for The Royal Diviner of The Oba:

The royal diviner of the Oba was responsible for making daily divination at the palace. He habitually made divination for himself before going to the palace. One day, the Royal diviner went to

Orunmila for divination, who advised him to serve his own Ifa with a crown, agbada gown, and beads, and to give a he-goat to Esu.

Instead of spending his own money to buy the materials, he decided to procure them from the Oba through stratagem. At his next daily divination for the Oba, he enumerated a number of things which the Oba should forbid. He also prescribed sacrifice with a crown, gown, beads and he-goat. The Oba provided the materials and he took them home for his own sacrifice.

As if his treachery was not bad enough, he began to boast at the instigation of Esu, that there was nothing the Oba had, which he did not have. When the chiefs were hearing about his boasting, they demanded explanations from the Oba. The Oba told them not to worry. He subsequently invited Orunmila for divination after which he was told to serve Esu with a he-goat, adding a dress made with the leaves of the plantain plant, so that Esu would return the properties trickishly taken from him. The Oba made the sacrifice.

After eating his he-goat, Esu backed a "sick" child and went to the house of the royal diviner to appeal to him to save the life of the child. He succeeded in saving the life of the child. The following day, Esu came to him to lend him the use of his regal gown, crown and beads to attend a conference to which he was invited. He willingly agreed to oblige. Meanwhile, Esu alerted the Oba to plant palace policemen to arrest him (Esu) at a prearranged rendezvous.

When Esu got to that point, he was instantly arrested for the unauthorized use of regal paraphernalia and appurtenances. That is how the materials were returned to the Oba and the royal diviner's appointment was terminated.

When this Ifa appears at Ugbodu, the person will be advised to beware of over-sympathizing with anyone, because excessive benevolence can bring him down from grace to grass. He should also be advised to refrain from boasting. He should serve the new Ifa with a white goat, white hen, and white kola nuts. He should forbid giving out any domestic bird or animal for rearing. He should also serve Esu with a he-goat and a basket filter and beads. At divination the person should be advised to serve Esu with a he-goat to avert the risk of paying dearly for excessive magnanimity. He or she should forbid having a light-complexioned spouse, and refrain from drinking in public.

Divined for Asehin When He wanted To Initiate His Wife To The Oro Cult:

Ti o ba ri aiye je tan, iwas ibaje nia nhu.

When one has made it materially in life, there is a tendency to become morally depraved. That was the name of the Ifa priest who made divination for high chief Asehin when he wanted to have his wife initiated into the Oro cult, inspite of the fact that women were traditionally prohibited from initiation. He was advised to make sacrifice with his chair, his wearing garment and a ram, but he refused to make the sacrifice. His favorite wife had been itching to know the secret of the Oro cult, but the Oloja always told her that women were forbidden to see the secrets of Oro.

When it was time for the annual festival of Oro, the woman renewed her request to see Oro. On the account of Chief Asehin's failure to make sacrifice, Esu was determined to expose him to ridicule and embarrassment. Acting under the guise of a visiting seer, Esu told him that his favorite wife had made a request to him, which he had been turning down. The seer told him that to avoid the risk of losing his favorite wife, he should build a special basket chair equipped with a space below it that it could accommodate a person. On the festival day, his wife was to occupy that space while he covered it with his flowing robes so that she could see what was happening. Chief Asehin fell easily for the strategy.

On the festival day, the chair was carried by his servants to the venue, covered with lace materials. As the Head chief of the town, Chief Asehin was required to light the torch that would mark the commencement of the ceremonies. The first visible indication that something had gone wrong was when the light refused to ignite and endure. After trying in vain to put on the light, he told the criers to proceed with the next stage of beating drums for Oro to get possessed and to appear to declare the curfew. The drummers beat the drum for several hours, but Oro did not get possessed. That was the confirmation that things had gone wrong somewhere. The chief priest of the cult subsequently sent errands to Orunmila for divination to find out the cause of the mishap.

They were all astonished by the subsequent revelation that the Head Chief himself had profaned the ceremonies by procuring a sacrilegious spy on the goings-on. That was why the ceremonies had forcibly applied brakes until the impious action of the Oloja was corrected. In fact, Orunmila insisted that the chair on which the Oloja was sitting should be examined, if he refused to own up.

When the errand-men got back to the Chief Priest, they announced their findings with a sarcastic song:

Bi ko dun, a o ye apere Oba wo

Meaning:

Let us call on Oro to appear once more,
But if he refused to appear,
we have to examine the basket-seat of the Oloja,
Because it appears to conceal a profane spy.

When indeed the criers again called on Oro to appear, he refused to respond. The Oloja, Chief Asehin was then approached to own up to the cause of the abortive developments. When he did not say anything positive; he was forced out from his seat and people were astonished to see that he had concealed a woman under the seat. The woman was immediately apprehended and made to go on her knees, where she was instantly besieged by soldier ants and wild bees which beat her to death. At the same time, chief Asehin was instantly banished from the throne.

When this odu appears at divination, the person will be advised to make prescribed sacrifices to avert the danger of the sudden death of his wife. If it appears for a woman, she will be warned not to take undue advantage of her husband's love to demand favors fraught with fatal consequences for herself and her husband.

This Odu's Special Sacrifice for Prosperity:

Orunmila declared that the corridor of his Father's (God's) house was lined with prosperity. His followers asked him what to do to avail themselves of the goodies lying on the corridor of his father's house.

He declared that it would require sacrifice to be slammed down on the corridor with coconut to serve the head. Thereafter all the instruments of prosperity, money, marriage and childbirth would come within the reach of the person making the sacrifice.

When it appears at divination, the person will be advised that his prosperity lies in his father's house in the land of his birth. He should not travel outside his home-base in quest of prosperity, because the consequences would be regrettable. He should stay at home.

Index

Ancient Wisdom of the Yorubas

from Athelia Henrietta Press

PUBLISHING IN THE NAME OF ÒRÚNMÌLÀ

- **Abimbola, 'Wande**
Ifa: An Exposition of Ifa Literary Corpus
256pp.   Illust. $24.95
- **Awolalu, J. Omosade**
Yoruba Beliefs and Sacrificial Rites 203pp.
Illust. $19.95
- **Buckley, Anthony D.**
Yoruba Medicine 224pp. $24.95
- **Elebuibon, Chief Ifayemi, Awise of Oshogbo**
Apetebii: The Wife of Òrúnmìlà 82pp. Illust.
$12.95
- **Farrow, Stephen S.**
Faith, Fancies and Fetiche 224pp. Illust.
$20.00
- **Ibie, C. Osamaro**
Ifism: The Complete Works of Òrúnmìlà
Vol. 1-The Sixteen Olodus 251pp. Illust.
Cloth $40.00
- **Ibie, C. Osamaro**
Ifism: The Complete Works of Òrúnmìlà
Vol. 2-The Odus of Eji-Ogbè How man created
his own God 242pp. Illust. $40.00
- **Ibie, C. Osamaro**
Ifism: The Complete Works of Òrúnmìlà
Vol. 3-The Odus of Oyeku-Meji 101pp. $25.00

The Yorùbá Center Inc.

High Quality Audio and Video Cassettes

AUDIO CASSETTES
EGBÉ OMO ANAGO MUSIC SERIES
Yorùbá Religious Music From Nigeria

OBATALA
Performed by Ishenbaiye, featuring Igbin and Dun Dun drums and praise songs to the King of White Cloth.

SANGO
Performed by Ishenbaiye, featuring Bata, Dun Dun, Shekere and praise singing to the divinity of thunder.

OSUN
Performed by Ishenbaiye, featuring Dun Dun, Shekere and praise songs to the river deity.

OGUN
Performed by Ishenbaiye, featuring Bata, Dun Dun, Shekere and praise songs for the divinity of Iron.

VIDEO CASSETTES
EGBÉ OMO ANAGO VIDEO SERIES
Yorùbá and Bantu Religious Videos From Cuba

ACHE MOYUBA ORISHA
A documentary that discovers the fascinating and mythical world of the Yorùbá religion in Cuba. Approx. 1 Hr. Spanish

EN EL PAIS DE LOS ORICHAS
A documentary on the Yorùbá religion (Santeria) and Rumba. Approx. 1 Hr. Spanish

NGANGA KIYANGALA
A deep look into the roots of Congo religion, of Bantu origin called Palo Monte. Approx. 1 Hr. Spanish

OGGUN
A documentary featuring "Akpon" Lazaro Ross on the Yorùbá religion-Santeria. The songs, dances, rites and altars. Approx. 1 Hr. Spanish